PARENTING THE ENLIGHTENED CHILD

A Handbook for revealing
and guiding the Spiritual Child

By
Alyce Bartholomew Soden

Copyright © 1997 Alyce Bartholomew Soden

All Rights Reserved by Author
Fish Rock Publications
Gualala, CA 95445
(707) 884-3631—(707) 884-3630 (fax)

No part of this book may be reproduced or transmitted in any form or by any means, electronic, mechanical, including photocopying, recording, or by any information storage and retrieval system, except in the case of reviews, without the express written permission of the publisher, except where permitted by law.

ISBN Number 1-57087-356-9

Professional Press
Chapel Hill, NC 27515-4371

Manufactured in the United States of America
97 98 99 00 00   1 2 3 4 5 6 7 8 8 10

Introduction

We entertain angels unaware. Every child is a Spiritual Being. Children are God's pure ideas coming unadulterated into this world. All beloved children of God come trailing clouds of glory in their wake.

I believe that one reason we parents dread our children's growing up is that we don't want them to lose the qualities of being that make us feel closer to Heaven when in their presence. Life is not a hit or miss proposition when we prepare adequately for any possible experience and continue to know who we are and why we're here. It is to carry the Light of Spirit forward uplifting the consciousness level of the earth. The kingdom of heaven which is within each of us will be the consciousness of the people here on earth. Is it too much to declare this as a reality. NEVER! Our children and our children's children are come to bring this about. No doubt they will do their best, and we can assist greatly by preparing them for their magnificent mission.

PREFACE

Having searched for the Truth and having devoted a lifetime of study to metaphysics, psychology, parapsychology, science, philosophy, mysticism, the esoteric and religion, I have difficulty remembering where I discovered this jewel of thought or that pearl of great price. With deep humility and thankfulness for those giants who have gone before, I beg their pardon if credit is not always given.

Due to the limitations of our language, I use the traditional form to include all people- no matter their gender.

DEDICATION

These mystical, insightful ideas and experiences have blessed our family and friends throughout the years. I trust they will do the same for you.

I dedicate this book to those who lived it with me.

TABLE OF CONTENTS

Chapter 1 Enlightened Souls..........1
Chapter 2 The World..........7
Chapter 3 The Child..........13
Chapter 4 Childhood is a Precious Time..........20
Chapter 5 Honey, We're Going to Have a Baby 28
Chapter 6 Stages and Stages..........36
Chapter 7 Stepping Out Into the World..........42
Chapter 8 Goal: Being a Fountain of Love......54
Chapter 9 Goal Setting..........64
Chapter 10 Levels of Soul Development..........72
Chapter 11 On Healing Your Child..........79
Chapter 12 Mastering Life..........91
Chapter 13 The Law of Belief..........102
Chapter 14 Purpose of Life..........117
Chapter 15 Prayer and Meditation..........123
Chapter 16 Using the Law of Visualization......134
Chapter 17 Further Questions..........143
Bibliography..........160

"It would be wonderful indeed if a group of people should arrive on Earth who were for something and against nothing."

(E.Holmes)

Chapter 1

ENLIGHTENED SOULS

Enlightened souls are now being born in large numbers everywhere on earth to herald in the year 2000. A higher level of consciousness is already surfacing that will bring peace, plenty, and improved life on this planet. With careful guidance by awakened parents, multitudes of children will avoid the pitfalls of the world and be ready to carry the Light onward to future generations.

It is time we look at our children with new eyes. We have discovered who and what we are as adults: divine children of a loving beneficent Father/Mother God. It is time to discover who these children are who are being birthed at this special time of the millennium?

Each new life enters the world with a divine potential. He is not ignorant of spiritual matters. In fact the younger the child the more knowledgeable he is of God, Life, Truth, Love and Beauty. We do not have to teach children any metaphysical truth. We merely need to remind them.

Every experience in life is a lesson to be recognized and searched for the blessing it contains. To know this truth is to look at life through new eyes, fearless and unafraid.

Numerous children from metaphysical homes where their divine sonship is recognized are ready for greater demands and expectations.

The sacred commitment of parenting a child of great potential demands that one set an example of the highest quality and prepare the child with knowledge of his divinity and high purpose in this incarnation. The child has already committed himself to a life of service to God and man. Parents, your task as an important way shower is already set between you and your child.

What attributes do you want your child to have? Do you want him to be peaceful, loving, generous, to make promises and keep them, to be dependable, persevering, forgiving?

BE THE EXAMPLE!

If you wish these or any other qualities, you must set a plan into motion that assures this automatic result. The old saying " An apple doesn't fall far from the tree," is infinitely probable in this case. So, parents must with conscious thought and effort BE what they want their child to emulate, because that will truly happen.

Parent and child are connected by contracts made before the parents' birth to provide the kind of life required for the child's greatest growth, for furthering his contribution to the consciousness of this planet.

Vast multitudes of new incarnates called "earth walkers" are bound to the physical level and incarnate repeatedly in whatever womb is available without question. These can be freed or free themselves from this circle by refusing addictions, releasing their former bonds by overcoming them, seeking their true identity, and recognizing their divinity.

Earth walkers incarnated at this time can be enlightened souls to a degree and are here in this schoolroom to expand their consciousness and support the overall good of the planet.

HOW DO YOU KNOW IF YOUR CHILD IS AN ENLIGHTENED SOUL?

The very fact that you are asking indicates something. You, yourself, are a seeker on the pathway or you would not be reading this book. Any soul incarnated within your sphere of influence has earned the right in prior incarnations, knowing that the example, education, training and awareness are available from YOU!

SO DON'T HIDE YOUR BELIEFS UNDER A BASKET OR KEEP YOUR LIPS SEALED OF YOUR KNOWLEDGE. Share with them the Truth revealed to you. Speak freely. Do not wait until they ask; do not wait out of fear that someone might disagree with you: a spouse, in-laws, or the traditional church. Start early in life, or begin at whatever age they are now.

Perhaps your child has exhibited great powers, such as clairvoyant, clairaudient, or ability to change matter-as many Japanese children did when witnessing a spoon being bent by mental power on TV. They turned and did the same.

If your child has an imaginary friend, sees colors around people, has a musical gift, or delights in the things of the Spirit, all these and many more are indications of enlightenment. Any child who has earned the right to be born in the United States of America at this time has reason enough to be suspected of being an enlightened, or old, soul.

WHO ARE THE PARENTS?

WHO SHOULD DO THE PARENTING?   YOU!

You who are seeking are an avenue of God's Good. Someone within your sphere of influence is awaiting a word, the Truth, to know of his divine heritage and be awakened again to his important role in this life. You influence some child even if it's only the paperboy. Speak when it's in you to be the channel. Speak!

We have read that individuals have many Guides on the other side during a lifetime to instruct and protect the precious seed. I am saying now that living Guides here on earth are provided for the same reason and to benefit soul growth.

Recognizing and accepting your commitment as parent, teacher, Guide and or advisor is a necessity.

We shall discover why certain negative traits appear at an early age and are seemingly difficult to overcome unless the child is carefully guided. We shall explore the lessons of overcoming the negative effects of the world and how to develop the perseverance to continue on this quest without losing sight of the goal.

The most important person in the life of the child you have contracted to guide IS YOU, THE GUIDE. Know this and act accordingly.

During the course of this book we will be dealing with life on three levels:

1. the physical level- living in the body, living the world today;

2. the mental world- living in our mental houses, experiencing race consciousness, ideas, conditions and beliefs of the world, learning to understand and use the physical laws;

3. the spiritual level- experiencing the spiritual level, using the Universal Power, trusting the Universal Presence and adhering to the Spiritual Laws.

All three levels are important. None can be skipped.

THE CHALLENGE

THE CHALLENGE RESTS WITH YOU, the Guide and teacher. Whether you are the natural parent, grandparent, related by blood or not, you know who you are in relationship to this child. Know that divine wisdom and divine guidance are ever present when teaching this child. It is not your meager wisdom that you must rely upon. You are eternally supported and guided in this matter. Consider this task an honor and privilege awarded in recognition of your enlightenment, and pursue it with great commitment and perseverance.

Keep in mind the purpose of ALL enlightened souls: THE RAISING OF THE CONSCIOUSNESS OF THE ENTIRE PLANET! Each individual soul has an important part to play toward that end.

For as each individualization grows in consciousness, his sphere of influence expands and other souls are lifted until all are raised in glory. Never underestimate the power of a single stone dropped into a pond. Its influence is felt over and over as the waves expand in circles around it.

So the CHALLENGE RESTS WITH YOU, the Guide and teacher. The purpose of this book is to assist you in your happy task. Be the great Spiritual Being that you are! Take your place as a Spiritual Guide and <u>eternally listen!</u>

"In the marathon of souls it is not the swiftest runners who win the race, but those who reach the goal with their torches still burning."(Corinne Heline)

Chapter 2

THE WORLD

The world we live in today is the result of generations of human beings stretching and straining to rise above their past level of consciousness. Mankind seems to advance and fall back, advance and fall back. Some parts of the world are seen to be largely unchanged since the Master Jesus walked: "An eye for an eye," and wars of revenge and retaliation continue. Peace and recognition treaties are occurring in the Middle East which are a positive sign of change. Ireland continues to fight the War of the Roses between Protestant and Catholics. Some are still fighting the American Civil War in this country. More recently, some are fighting the war of ideology, Democracy vs. Communism.

The battles fought between Science and Religion are still prevalent in some minds today. Traditional religion has not kept up with the developments of science and demands that its adherents accept its dogma " on faith."

The world has become smaller resulting from recent technological advancement. Each individual entity has greater influence than ever before on the evolving consciousness of the earth. Children are being brought from Ireland, where the War continues and are given the opportunity to experience a place where both Catholic and Protestant can live in peace side by side. Children are being adopted from Africa, Asia, South America and many other parts of the world that are in conflict. These children are being raised in this country of freedom and some will return to their native land filled with new possibilities and eagerly bring them about.

A number of today's leaders of Third World countries were educated in the free world. Boys from the Palestine Liberation Organization and Israel were sent to camp together in this country as a peace treaty was being negotiated. Youngsters who may be fighting each other were given the opportunity to become friends.

CRISIS AT HOME, TOO

Yet our country with it's broader view is facing a crisis of great proportions as our greatest national resource our youth, are being limited, stained and diverted in three major ways:

First, drug abuse is affecting many of our young people though education is slowly making inroads into changing peoples minds about it. An eight year old related to me that his teenage brother had just killed himself. He was high on drugs and rode his bicycle head on into an oncoming car. Jorge said," I'm not going to end up on the garbage heap like my brother." and he didn't. He is now married and studying law.

The second obsession is alcohol abuse. Some children at age twelve are addicted partly because we as adults have carelessly made it available in our homes. Our obsessive Friday night parties have been carried to the extreme. It is noteworthy that alcohol is rarely advertised on TV and responsible drinking is being stressed by the major producers of alcoholic beverages. We are showing that we can overcome even the greatest limitations. It is always our choice.

Education is slowly making inroads into changing peoples minds about drugs and alcohol. We are thankful for Presidential leadership in this matter.

It may seem to some that a discussion of the challenges our youth experience in the world is out of place in the spiritual view. We do live in the world and as a result are influenced by world thought. We have the power to change even the most reprehensible, the most devastating and debilitating challenges we face. Leadership on many levels, heroes of today, living Guides and those on the other side working together are making a change in our world.

This is why adult Guides that are incarnated in this parenthesis are being called to take a child 'under their wing,' so to speak, and assist them through the pitfalls so prevalent at this time in the world. YOU HAVE BEEN CALLED AND YOU ARE CHOSEN!

As Guides and teachers,we must assist them to respond on the mental level instead of the emotional level. My friends do it and it hasn't hurt them; instead on the mental level, what effect will drugs have on my body, and my world, with the consequent loss of one thinking, creating, expanding soul? What effect will drugs have on my purpose in this lifetime?

When actions stem from the mental level, the pressure of the peer group seems to fall on deaf ears. Our regular and consistent support needs to be implemented from as early as eight years of age.

The church has provided activities for its young people for generations, and remains its responsibility. An active, positive youth organization is a strong deterrent to the influence of the addiction oriented world consciousness.

The fourth crisis is the trend to single parent families. A large percentage of our homes are stressed beyond capacity with only one working adult, often alone, trying to be both mother and father with much less earning capacity, they are living in abject poverty. Many children are deprived of the knowledge of the masculine influence.

The fifth crisis is unwise and irresponsible sexual experience. A recent study shows that many very young girls are impregnated by much older men in her innocence and as an initiation into a gang, Our girls are limited and derailed from the higher path; babies having babies is a sad note of our times. In the rush to"grow up" or to be in the "in" group, many lives are being limited. Isn't it interesting that AIDS and herpes have come also at this time? and that there is as yet no cure for either. The general thought on the street is that "it won't happen to me." So, youth continue to play Russian Roulette with their lives.

The Law when you play with fire, you will get burned will cause many a sad, limited life to be experienced unnecessarily. Prevention, early planning, and open communication are the very best deterrents.

I do not believe " whatever will be will be." This has been a cop out for generations. I do believe that a pound of prevention is worth more than a pound of cure. Let's assist our youth in avoiding the pitfalls of growing up in this world.

WHAT ABOUT TODAY'S CHILDREN ?

Today's children are the children of the unchurched, a secular society. Up to the end of the 1800's, the Church was the greatest influence on the family and most individual lives. To be a Church member and supporter was expected. To be a "God fearing man" was a badge of honor. For various reasons the Church influence has eroded to a mishmash of remembered dogma and is no longer a viable influence in this secular society. Few children are given spiritual or religious training, and generally do not know where to turn when faced with any kind of problem. The strength of the family unit has been undermined. The moral fiber has been overcome by a generation of "if it feels good, do it" attitude with no regard to the consequences. The results are ruined lives, addicted bodies and limited minds. The cry for a return to moral values is beginning to be heard throughout the land.

I am the first one to disclaim that we must return to the ways of our fathers. Going back is never a solution. Going forward taking the good that has evolved through it all: women's rights, children's rights, freedoms of all kinds, learning to love and accept every person regardless of race, creed, color, gender or sexual preference. These are definite advancements made recently by human kind on the physical level.

Because our world has become smaller as man's technology has advanced, the result is an intermingling of Eastern and Western values and life styles, and the old ways are generally left behind. The Western cultures shy away from the Eastern influence and vice versa, but the inevitable result is a blending together, hopefully of the best of both. We are in a time of world-wide change. What will be the result? "One great step forward for mankind?" Today's children will be the deciders. What standards will they use for their vital decision making? It is a frightening picture to see a people returned to the values and laws of the old days, as the Ayatollah has inflicted upon Iran. But so also would be a return to the original Judeo-Christian mores of the Master Jesus' time, the Fourteenth century or even those of the Victorian era. We must march forward. Let's support today's children so they will have the tools to make wise decisions.

"The chalice of the Holy Grail within each one is connected in a flowing current of Universal Love around the whole circle of earth" (Corinne Heline)

Chapter 3

THE CHILD

Every child comes into this world surrounded by pure white light which protects and nurtures him.

EVERY CHILD IS TOTALLY SIN FREE! No taint or stigma surrounds his purity. Only the pure light of God surrounds a child until about the age of two years. At that time the child has begun to adjust to the body and is beginning to direct its ways to serve his purposes. From conception, the child is increasingly aware of the outside world, and it influences him to the degree that it serves his needs in preparing for the life he is to live particularly if there in a change of culture from his last incarnation.

According to Corinne Heline," the incoming ego remains in the aura of its chosen mother for about twenty-one days after conception has taken place, after which it enters the mother's body and begins to assist actively building its new vehicle. This it forms in complete harmony with the archetype pattern in higher realms. This archetype is fashioned in conformity with forces set into motion by the ego itself in previous lives upon earth."

The body with its mutually agreed upon traits is the earned or chosen vehicle of this lifetime. You may ask, " What about the deformed or mentally retarded child?" The quality of the body is fitted to the needs of the individual's experiences during any incarnation and cannot over ride natures law. Certainly natures law cannot be avoided. An infinite number of reasons are possible, but choice of body rests upon the incarnating soul. A soul just expanding to a higher level may choose a physical body that is limited in order to advance. Or a higher-level soul may need further experience in the physical level and agrees to a life of physical handicap to further his development. All incarnations are a result of choice. When Jesus was asked about the man who was born blind, he answered his disciples, "So that the works of God might be manifest in him."(John 9:3 Lamps trans.)

A handicapped woman shared why she chose this limited body in this life time, she answered, "I chose my mother. I wanted to be her child." The physical law that was in effect that this child would be physically challenged was not a consideration in this case. (Even the earth walkers have the choice but may not exercise it and many choose to return immediately to earthly life in whatever vehicle available).

At birth the aura of the child is pure white. It gradually takes on the physical-sexual level, and becomes red. The aura may remain mainly red the entire lifetime if the soul develops no further. Orange is the color of emotion. As the child develops, he may use emotion to get his needs met. The aura then contains red and orange, which indicated his physical, sexual and emotional levels. It is the task of the Guide to lead the child safely through the physical-sexual and emotional levels as carefully as possible and into the yellow of the mental level. No age is exempt from the influence of the physical- sexual or emotional level but it can and must come under the control of the mental. The mind must govern the lower senses in order to advance further. We all wear our badges of levels of consciousness for those discerning enough to see. When the level of mind over body, or metaphysical, is reached, the lesser levels remain, but are gradually overpowered by the yellow. We use the mental level frequently to overcome the lower states. As the child becomes more and more adept at using the mind to overcome problems of the physical-sexual and emotional levels, he is ready to acknowledge his divinity. Through his conscious use of his higher understanding, his life reflects his use of the Higher Power and his aura adds the green of service. Any level may represent a lifetime or many lifetimes of accomplishment, but the desire once stirred remains a goal to be fulfilled, carried forever in the pattern of the soul.

Blue, the color of Spiritual Awareness, is reached when the individual has overcome all lower states, but sparks of blue may indicate the soul's aspirations long before the level is reached and mastered. Blue indicates mastery of all levels below and is the bridge through indigo to purple. The level of the Master Jesus, the Christ, is white, glowing brilliant white, with all other colors represented as in a crystal.

In every lifetime the maximum is possible. However, most souls take many lifetimes to master each level. Through the schoolroom of earth, souls advance more quickly, but lengthy preparation has proceeded an incarnation of any enlightened soul. The child who exhibits giftedness at an early age in music, art or mathematics has had long and exacting training by the Masters on the other side.

Every child is a potential Christ in the making. What a wonderful opportunity that is!

TODAY'S CHILDREN

What about today"s children? Generally, they are of a higher native intelligence and able to master the steadily advancing academic levels required. They are physically less handicapped, as a result of advanced medicine, than any previous generation. They have greater opportunities through modern technology to know the world and beyond. But, the inner man has been sorely neglected. Honor, truth, honesty, steadfastness, purpose, self-discipline: many of the old virtues have been compromised or forgotten.

Every child is born with a divine spark hidden within him. This is not just the spark of life, which is given freely but the Inner Light of the Divine, God individualized, that is located in the innermost part of his being waiting for his awakening. I truly believe that everyone who is on a pathway toward enlightenment was an enlightened child from birth, put on this earth at this time in this place as a way shower. Many who have found their way later in life have said, " Oh, if I'd only known this sooner." Now is the time to make this happen for someone you know who is waiting.

It seems to me that in every incarnation we have to rediscover and relearn that we are Spiritual Beings, living in a Spiritual Universe, governed by the Spiritual Laws of Cause and Effect.

Some souls awaken to their Divinity as a result of some life experience, or out of pure curiosity, or by a word or example shown by an already awakened soul. Some never forget their Divinity as the Master Jesus, brought that knowledge with him consciously into this expression. Awakening to this realization is the most important purpose of life.

The Judeo-Christian belief that a child is born in sin has limited man's development for many thousands of years. It is long overdue that it be set aside.

ALL BABIES, NO MATTER THEIR SEX, COLOR, SITUATION OR PHYSICAL MAKEUP, ARE DIVINE, GOD INDIVIDUALIZED. Who can look into the eyes of a beautiful baby and not know this Truth?

When I was in the laundromat one day there was a baby lying awake and looking around in his car seat. An elderly gentleman approached the baby and gently took the baby's hand . Looking into the baby's face, he whispered,
" So you see the angels? You are so close to God, you see the angels. I am old and I don't see the angels anymore, but you see the angels."

Today's children have agreed to the Great Plan: to further man's inner development, to recognize mankind's Divinity, to further development of spiritual and moral values equal to the development of science and technology, and to bring peace, plenty and balance to this world.
It has always required only a few to change our world. Great hope is placed upon the shoulders of this generation. It is a tall order!

You may question how just a few can change this slow-moving earth. Remember the sixties? The Peace and Love Movement is still influencing this world, and now as adults have formed legitimate organizations such as Beyond War, Green Peace, and other conservationist and peace-fostering groups.

Of course many souls have committed themselves to further and to reveal the greatest cause in this lifetime: God in us, as us, is that which we are. Many will serve. Not all will be in the limelight, but they will nonetheless serve with benefit to themselves as they fulfill their commitment to the world in general.

You may ask, Why we are having a baby boom just now? Every available mother is being utilized to bring these enlightened souls into incarnation. The world is being prepared for their coming by the spiritual leaders here, now. The torch will be passed to those who have avoided the pitfalls of worldly life and are ready to accept the Light.

As a way shower, you are a living Guide. Your

task is to prepare as many of this generation as you can to carry the torch until it is time to relinquish it. Doing so brings joy and purpose into your life. You have been called and
YOU ARE CHOSEN.

Today's youth are bombarded with the consciousness of the world before birth. Much is learned within the womb to prepare the incarnating soul to accelerate adjustment into this world. The time in the womb is well spent on all levels, not just for the development of the unconscious.

Revealing the True self to the self is the most important step on life's pathway. The spark of God discovered individually raises all humanity.

Luke 2:52 "And Jesus grew in his stature and his wisdom, and favor with God and men."

Chapter 4

CHILDHOOD IS A PRECIOUS TIME

Childhood is a precious time. Productively spent, it can shape a life worthy of its purpose to prepare the soul to take its place carrying the Light. Quiet time, thoughtful time, day-dreaming time, singing praises to God, or time spent in spiritual discourse have great value.

What traits are present in children that appear to be lost as the child enters adulthood? Before the debilitating effects of the world consciousness, the child is loving unconditionally, forgiving, innocent and without guile, seeing with clear vision but without truly understanding both where he has come from or the place he has now entered. His trust without question, is open and receptive; he is teachable. This naivete is true of the inner man. The Kingdom of Heaven is made up of this level of consciousness.

When we are able to carry these attributes of being into adult life, the world consciousness is raised. As the Master Jesus said, "Truly I say to you, Whoever does not receive the kingdom of God like a little child shall not enter it..."(Mark 10:16 Lampsa trans.)

Many lessons must be learned, a foundation of solid belief in God must be laid and methods of meeting the world's challenges must become an automatic response before the teenage years arrive. Scientific Prayer Treatment, meditation and the inner listening for direction will supply that foundation.

I believe that one reason we parents dread our children's growing up is that we don't want them to lose the qualities of being that make us feel closer to Heaven when in their presence. Life is not a hit or miss proposition when we prepare adequately for any possible experience and continue to know who we are and why we're here. It is to carry the Light of Spirit forward uplifting the consciousness level of the earth. The kingdom of heaven which is within each of us will be the consciousness of the people here on earth. Is it too much to declare this as a reality. NEVER! Our children and our children's children are come to bring this about. No doubt they will do their best, and we can assist greatly by preparing them for their magnificent mission.

DEVELOPING DEDICATION OF PURPOSE:

SELF DISCIPLINE

Each child born to the earth comes with one or more purposes. Individually, his purpose is to grow and develop to his greatest potential, to develop his God-given talents and learn to use Universal Laws for his benefit. His greater commitment is to further God's purpose, which is to add to the steady upliftment of the earthly consciousness, and to raise the collective unconscious.

Certain Light Bearers are incarnated to further

God's plan. Who have been previously trained on the other side to perform certain tasks or assignments. Every mother's wish is to bear a child of this caliber. But the qualifications of the parents must be of the highest level. So to bear a soul already dedicated to a purpose is usually given to an old soul and/or one who him or herself carries the Light. Many times a family will incarnate in sequence: Light Bearer will birth a Light Bearer who will then birth a Light Bearer, each knowing his or her special purpose and the important contribution to be made.

The mystic sage, Emerson, said; "When a child comes forth from its mother's womb, the gate of gifts closes behind it." And Corrine Helene concurs with, "To a woman who learns to surround herself and fill her consciousness with only the good, the beautiful and the true, an unworthy ego cannot come; the strength of her love and aspiration will draw to her, unerringly, one who is worthy of her ideals,"(New Age Bible Interpretation Part I Chap. I), God is truly working Its purpose out, through US.

Every individual's plan, no matter the degree of spiritual attainment, is to become God-like.

With each incarnation the basic desire is always the same, to be a true example of God and to awaken the Divine Spark within. This is individually written in the Divine Intuition awaiting its recognition.

Each lifetime holds its lessons and potential for development. Even the severely handicapped person, whether physically or mentally, has a potential for great development. Lessons are presented over and over until mastered.

One man at the age of 50 was again presented an opportunity to get a college education. The opportunity, he admits was presented previously but was not acted upon. This time he followed through. He was amazed at his mental ability when he took the College Entrance Exam and passed it. He always had that potential.

Every child is born with important purposes to fulfill, but the self-discipline required to attain that purpose largely has to be developed here. Lessons in self-discipline begin at the mother's breast when the child's teeth are coming in, and he discovers that biting is not acceptable behavior. It may take a few times but the lesson is finally learned. It would be nice if each lesson was learned forever, but that appears not to be the case.

It has been my observation that lessons must be experienced again and again before learning takes place. One learning does not always apply to another. Self-discipline is necessary to perform most tasks agreed upon. AGREED UPON? Yes, agreed upon. Before birth each soul is given the opportunity of previewing the potential for a single life incarnation. Having viewed the Akashic Records where each one's eternal life records are kept, it is possible to know of the levels of consciousness attained, habits, challenges, debts, additions, and any karmic liabilities still to overcome.

The soul knows what is required and in viewing

the potential of the available incarnation will accept it or reject it. Also, contracts are made with the children to be born in that incarnation. All is agreed upon before the birth of the parent. Freedom of choice is enacted before birth, and then the freedom of choice continues through out that lifetime.

The successful fulfillment of that contract is often based on the amount of self-discipline developed. " Many are called, but few are chosen." (Matt. 22:14) And fewer still fulfill the assignment. When it is an important task, many are prepared, and several are committed to the task. The telephone was invented the same day by Alexander Graham Bell and Elisha Gray. The telephone's day had come and several were sent to present it to the world. Only a few actually accomplished the task.

So you ask Why do I have to live up to my commitment in any lifetime? Of course you don't, but in many cases you get the opportunity to do it again and again in that lifetime, or try again in another lifetime. Then too, you may get to learn to live up to your commitments, by experiencing the betrayal of someone dear to you who does not live up to his/her commitments, such as a marriage contract. This is very painful.

How do you become aware of the great service you have to provide in this life time? How do you know what service your child has to provide in his lifetime.? Many times this information comes through dreams or meditation or may be revealed by an awake psychic friend or relative.

Parents often know, the mother particularly. As the Mother Mary knew when she was told by the Angel Gabriel.

The childs' play activities at an early age may reveal his purpose. An ancient Oriental test is given at the child's first birthday. A number of articles symbolic of the different life choices a person could choose are placed on the floor around the infant. The one he crawls to and picks up is noted as his chosen profession, and he is trained in that direction. The choice is revealed. If the child goes from one to the other without a clear choice, the parents do it for him.

It is said of old that when Moses was presented by his adopted mother, the sister of the Pharaoh at court, her brother was quite willing to accept him as her own, but he worried that sometime this nephew might attempt to overthrow him or usurp his power. He commanded that a test be made. He put tiny Moses on the floor. On one side he put his crown and on the other he put a live coal that was glowing red hot. Moses started to crawl toward the crown but someone nearby intervened and he changed direction. When he reached for the coal it burned his hand and he put his hand into his mouth which burned his tongue. As a result, he was never able to speak clearly. It was understood that had Moses chosen the crown, he would have been killed immediately.

Our direction is often revealed in a recurring dream or a gnawing intuition that comes repeatedly saying," Be a minister," or " Be a scientist," or "Be a musician." The freedom is so great that one may never heed the call and nothing comes of it. The choice may be revealed by a strong interest or talent displayed in childhood or an attachment to some other person's profession out of respect for that person.

HOW TO DEVELOP SELF-DISCIPLINE IN YOUR CHILD.

Self-discipline is mandatory to performing the life task. The school experience provides graduated steps vital in developing self-discipline The clues given the teacher in kindergarten as she views the development of the child are: the child stays with a task until he finishes it, he sees the value of the work done and is proud when the work is completed, he may even 'see' the task in its final form when he is just starting to work on it.

Parents can encourage self-discipline in the home. First, by acknowledging with enthusiasm your child's beginning attempts to complete a task: picking up toys, putting a puzzle together, putting a book back in its place on the shelf, tying his shoes or taking himself to the bathroom on time, all are indicators of self-discipline. When the child begins to keep his room in order or helps do some of the household tasks, it should be noted.

Second, regular responsibilities should begin when the child is of school age. At first they should be centered around his own needs: to dress himself, keep his room in order, and brush his teeth. As these are mastered without reminders, more should be added. By the time the child is seven, the responsibilities should include some that serve others or support the families needs: setting and/or clearing the table, taking out the trash, feeding and caring for a pet, and bringing home notices from school. If the child seems to have difficulty doing all the tasks expected, the parent can make a chart and hang it on the back of the bedroom door with each job listed and the day and time it needs to be done. Every time the child remembers and does the task without reminder, the parent puts a star on the chart. When the agreed number of tasks are done, a special privilege or treat can be the reward.

A third way to develop self-discipline in your child is naturally provided in certain studies or disciplines, such as music, mathematics or science. Learning to play an instrument is often put off until the child shows an interest instead of starting the lesson of self-discipline early and as an important part of his education. The child's interest should be taken into account when he has mastered the instrument to some degree.

I Corinthians 15:49 And as we have borne the image of the earthy, shall also bear the image of the heavenly.

Chapter 5

HONEY, WE'RE GOING TO HAVE A BABY

Have you longed to hear these words? Have you longed to say these words? Many people have. Sometimes they are long in coming or something happens during the pregnancy and the baby never materializes. It is also reassuring to know that one does not have to be a parent in every lifetime. No doubt the next life experience will be different in this regard.

A couple I know tried for years to conceive to no avail. They sought medical assistance and still were not successful. Finally, they decided to adopt. The father confided in me that in order to make them appear as more acceptable parents to the agency, he got his long flowing mane of red hair cut and trimmed his beard, stopped smoking and drinking beer. They were just going to make an appointment to have their picture taken for their application, when the fertility drug the wife was taking took affect and they were pregnant. This time, the doctor thought it was normal. And it was. A beautiful baby girl was the result.

Many changes had to occur in the personality and life style of this couple before they were suitable vessels to nurture the elevated soul given into their care. Their longing and desire was not sufficient.

More and more mothers are abstaining from drugs (even prescribed drugs) as well as alcohol, tobacco, sugar, and carbonated drinks. They are also avoiding negative thoughts and unpleasant circumstances in order to bring about a healthy, happy and perfect child. Fathers, too, prepare by shaping up their lives and their habits.

It is recommended that both parents spend time in meditation from the moment that the idea crosses their mind to have a child in order to prepare themselves to be the greatest selves they can be. Prepare yourselves on the inner level of consciousness, and align yourselves in Spirit to the Universal God and prepare the physical world that this soul will enter, to the best of your ability.

REMEMBER: No one walks so tall as when he takes the hand of a child.

The circumstances that surround the developing fetus are very important as the hearing and emotional abilities are awakened at an early age. An account of John the Baptist is given in the New Testament: still in his mother Elizabeth's womb, he leaped at the sound of Mother Mary's voice as she greeted them.

A young family had a pet cockatoo that crowed all day long very loudly. When the baby was born, her cry was the same pitch and sounded just like the bird.

A father proudly revealed to me: He daily caressed his unborn baby and sang a little song. As the baby was being born, he sang the little song and his son turned his head, looked at him directly and smiled, then went on to his mother's breast. What a thrilling moment that was!

In an old Disney movie, <u>The Blue Bird of Happiness</u>, there is a beautiful scenario showing the returning souls being taken across the sea of clouds from Heaven in a sailboat. In the background are the voices of their awaiting mothers singing songs of welcome to them. Their attitudes about the life they are about to embark upon is explained. Each incoming soul has fore knowledge of the life he is about to live and is well prepared to be successful in it.

To be successful though, the child needs more caring and nurturing than just that of the natural parents and grandparents. He needs the kindness and understanding of adults with whom he comes in close contact, for instance a lady who lives next door who cleaned the tar off the refrigerator in her garage that your four year old painted so happily one afternoon when you thought you knew just where he was and what he was doing. Or the man who gave him his first pony ride, free.

Many people will act in a parenting manner to your child as he grows up. Some you wish they did not, but as with adults, the Law functions the same with children. We all draw to us people and experiences that we need in order to fulfill our purpose in this life.

It is the responsibility of all adults to set the example and reach out their hands to the youth who are struggling to find their way in the maze called life.

TREASURE MAP YOUR BABY TO ORDER

It may seem that conceiving, building and developing a fetus is a hit or miss situation, though mathematicians have computed the odds down to a "gnat's eyebrow". Truly, it has gone on for many thousands of years with man's understanding of the process still very limited.

Treasure Mapping is a successful method of reducing this uncertainty. The child is formed in the mind of the parents, mainly the mother and together the incoming soul and the parents build the instrument. The father's role is to provide a consistent harmonious atmosphere supporting the mother's physical needs and responsibility. It is not unheard of for the mother to dream clear pictures of her unborn child. The life situation, beliefs and attitudes of the parents affect the formation of the child physically, mentally, emotionally and spiritually. The mental and emotional state, the whole climate of the home is important to the developing fetus.

At this time it is propitious that the mother step out of the fast lane of worldly affairs, meditate daily, listen to beautiful music and think good, beautiful and true thoughts. It is recorded that the Mother Mary and Mother Elizabeth (mother of John, the Baptist) withdrew to a rural place while carrying their sons.

Treasure Mapping is a method of directing the mind of the individual repeatedly toward a desired result until the pattern is well set in consciousness and becomes demonstrated in physical form. Universal Mind is the power that sets into motion the pattern presented.

1. Families have used this method for many years. My grandmother wanted a red-haired, blue-eyed girl for her fourth baby so she attached a picture of her choice on the inside of the wood-box lid. Every time she took out wood for her cook stove she saw the picture and reaffirmed her desire. She had her red-haired girl. Later, she tried it again with a blond. It worked then, too.

Already having a tall, brown eyed, brown-haired girl, one couple found a picture of a blond, blue-eyed, light-framed girl and placed it on their Treasure Map. Every time they passed it they thanked God for their perfect, beautiful daughter, and they received her just as ordered. She resembled very closely the picture they had visually and mentally patterned.

For the next child they desired a boy. As they listened closely, the name they had chosen for him was not acceptable. So they went over their list again and again until they felt comfortable with it. There were times when they felt a strong influence of the incoming soul. In fact he dominated the Treasure Map so completely that they removed everything not related to him. Listening intuitively added much excitement and pleasure not usually attend a birth.

If your goal is to birth a highly-evolved soul as it was with the parents in ancient Hebrew times, you have to be willing to put up with all kinds of "not normal" problems. The Master Jesus' parents lost their privacy as Jesus' bath water, his clothing, and blankets were reputed to have great healing properties.

It was reported that Bartholomew was dying. His mother obtained the bath water from the Mother Mary, bathed him in it and wrapped him in Jesus' blanket and he was healed. Bartholomew later became a disciple.

If you were a parent of a child who could do magic or miracles from an early age, how would you feel trying to guide him to use those powers in a beneficial manner? Ancient manuscripts indicate that Mary and Joseph had just such a challenge.

HOW TO TREASURE MAP YOUR CHILD TO ORDER:

Step 1. Decide exactly what you both want. Visualize exactly what you desire the physical body to be: the sex, coloring, body shape and health. It is even possible to design the personality traits, interests and life pattern if you desire. You can go even further and design the life pattern if you so desire. Frank Lloyd Wright's mother desired an architect and got exactly what she wanted (according to his biography).

Step 2. Find a picture of just such a new-born.

Step 3. Decide which form of Treasure Map to use: notebook, poster, wheel, or another. Having the Map posted in a prominent place for all to see is beneficial.

Step 4. Decide the mental capacity, emotional qualities, interests, talents, and any other vision you have regarding the incoming soul. Place words describing him around the picture.

Step 5. Decide on the circumstances of birth and ease of delivery; make a place; prepare other family members and project the mother's perfect physical well-being. Prepare the consciousness of the family to accept with love, peace and joy this blessed child.

Step 6. Request the highest level of spiritual being available.

Step 7. Prepare yourselves in physical, mental, emotional and spiritual ways to receive your desire (both parents). Expect it to be so.

Step 8. Meditate, pray, listen for direction and follow it.

Step 9. Put words of praise and thanksgiving to God all around the edges of the Map and know that the incoming soul will glorify

God to the highest degree.

Step 10. Every time you think of this wonderful event or pass the Treasure Map, thank God for the perfect action of Spirit that is taking place.

Step 11. Expect all the money needed for expenses to be provided in an easy way.

Step 12. Expect all to be in perfect order: perfect time, perfect place, perfect child and perfect circumstances.

Families have been very successful using this method.

Treasure Mapping is a well known, time tested method of visual prayer. Know that each time you put your attention to it, it is a prayer. It is also a pattern being set in Mind which will be manifested. Clear thinking at this time is important. Confusion will bring about a confused result. So be specific. With prayer and thanksgiving your desire will be honored.

..of Him and through Him, and to Him are all things.
Romans 11:36

Chapter 6

STAGES AND STAGES

It seems that life is just a series of stages. Some have called them "passages" in adult life, but they remain an attitude or form of action commonly experienced at a certain time in life.

ARE THE "TERRIBLE TWOS "THE FIRST " I WANT TO BE ME' STAGE?

This first step out for independence may be earth shaking to parents. It comes before they are ready. One moment they feel they have a perfectly darling dependable baby (part of me); the next moment they have a belligerent screaming monster. " What have I done? " is the first question." What shall I do about it?" is the next. What a frustrating time for parents. They are hardly used to having a child and now its antics are unbearable and often embarrassing.
"Can't you control your kid?" a passerby questions as your child stands there screaming for his own way, which is impossible.

If it will help any, we, who have raised children, understand.

Now, let us examine where the child is: He can walk, talk some and knows what he wants. His parents have given him everything he wants, sometimes before he wants it. So now he wants to run in the street. Or he wants no one else but his mother to carry him. Pregnant mother can hardly carry herself,but he wants or: NO, I won't go to the bathroom! The child is dancing about.

There are many ways the parents can meet these challenges. Usually, they are caught unaware and then meet them head on. "No! Stay out of the street or you will be run over by a car." Paddle, paddle! There is nothing wrong with this reaction. Some "Terrible Twos" balk on every issue, escalating the frustration.

What is a poor parent to do?

GET A PLAN! When the parents realize that force or being bigger isn't going to do it, then being smarter is the answer. When the parents learn that 'Do you want' will bring an automatic and resounding 'NO!' as a response, they will stop asking and instead take the child by the hand and do it. If this causes a negative response still, use your creativity. Grab up his Teddy Bear and say "Teddy has to go potty." Put Teddy on first, taking lots of time, then put the child on.This won't work every time so plan something different for the next time. Be creative. Avoid confrontation, unless it endangers life, limb or a family member. If you have to confront, be sure YOU WIN !This too will pass.

The hardest part of being a parent is to realize that this child is not your personal, private property. He was given through you for your care, not for your keeping. The 'Terrible Two's" may have purpose, may be for an awakening of the parents to this fact, and to help them release this little person who is in itself unfolding in its own individual way.

Try not to react to idle remarks of bystanders or what the neighbors say. You are the expert on this child. No one else knows him as you do, nor cares for him as you do. So do the best that you know how to do and let the rest pass. Do not carry guilt over what you should have done. Just resolve to do better next time.

THE HARDEST PART OF PARENTING IS TO LET GO----

> Let go when he is ready to walk alone. Let go when he knows how to do it himself at two. Let go when he goes to school. Let go when he's ready to go away to camp at seven. Let go when he's ready to ride his bike to the library at nine. Let go when... Let go when he's ready to get his driver's license. Let go on his first date. Let go when he goes away to college or gets married.   LET GO! Easiest words to say, but hard to do. The only solution that really works is to put him in "someone's" care. Put him in God's White Light of Protection and Guidance and   Let Go! That is what parents must do. YOU, THE PARENT: WHAT IS YOUR RELATIONSHIP WITH YOUR PARENTS?

On the scale from one to ten, ten being super, what is your relationship to your parents? Is it great, wonderful, loving, caring and responsive? Or not? Are you still speaking? Are you still fighting to be accepted as grown up? Are you over the they-did-me-wrong'attitude? Hopefully, you know they-did-the-best-they-knew-how under the conditions that existed in their lives and what they knew at that time.This usually comes when children become parents.

An interesting example came into view recently. The unwed teenage mother who chose to keep her child is not sending her to school,regularly. The mother is in her early twenties now and the child is seven. They still live with the mother's parents, and she's still fighting for her freedom.
The mother tried it on her own once but the she was only able work at fast food places and the pay was not enough to live on. Grandmother works, as she always has, to keep life and limb together. Grandfather is older, retired and an alcoholic. Battles rage constantly in this home over who is responsible for the child. The three adults in this home are acting like teenagers fighting one another. The child is neglected. She comes to school tardy, hungry and dirty or not at all. Mother is sleeping in, Grandpa is drunk and Grandma has already gone to work. Who is taking responsibility for raising this child?
Nobody! Grandma can't say anything or even help her with her math because her daughter will get mad. The mother is confused and still fighting everything, including the school. The child is raising herself.

You may be sure that whatever your situation is with your parents, you are passing it on to the next generation. You yourself will be treated the same way you treated your parents when your child grows up. We carry our childhood hurts and feelings well into adulthood, and many never lay them to rest.

Are you still embarrassed by your parents? Are you embarrassed by who they are and what they did or did not do? If you still harbor that feeling, it's time to overcome it, forgive and release.
DO NOT PASS IT ON. Do better with your own child!

We carry our hurts and disappointments of growing up well into adulthood and many people never come to grips with them. Modern psychiatry seems to continue the problem for years with no solution. Metaphysics has the best answer. FORGIVE!

Forgive! Forgive! This is what rebirthing is all about: Forgive from the moment of conception to the present day. Forgive each overt act, each covert act and the actions of omission. Forgive everyone, whether it be the doctor who birthed you, the older sibling who hit you on the head with a rake when you were three, the uncle who molested you, or the aunt who down-graded you. Whatever or who-ever it was, forgive them now and forever.

You may have wished you could communicate with those persons and tell them what they did to you. You can still write a letter to them, include all the hurtful feelings and anger that you still feel, release them and forgive them.
Write the letter only DON'T MAIL IT. BURN IT!
You will be freed from the burden and the experience with no repercussions. If you send it, you will just perpetuate the problem and perhaps escalate it out of proportion.

Another way of releasing that works well, whether the person is alive or dead, is a soliloquy in which you visualize the person you wish to communicate with and set him in a chair opposite you. Pick a time and place that you will not be disturbed or heard. Sit down and tell him what he did and how you feel about it. Rant and rave until you are freed from that problem. You may have to do it several times until you can forgive yourself and him. Do so and let it go.

It is said that you become an adult when you can forgive your parents.

I have been teaching elementary school for thirty-five years. I see a tremendous need for educating parents on how to be parents. I recommend that every thirteen-year-old be required to take a class in parenting and its responsibilities, with further instruction each year as he progresses in school. Such a class might reduce the number of children born to children or untrained, irresponsible, non-caring parents. Most parents are caring and well-meaning but are not prepared for the exacting challenges they will encounter.

We are all always going through stages. Understanding this about yourself makes relationships with family and friends easier and more understandable. Be patient with yourself and your children as they pursue adulthood.

"By the aid of self-control, resolution, purity, righteousness and well directed thought a man ascends."
As A Man Thinketh p.68

Chapter 7

STEPPING OUT IN THE WORLD

The transition from home to school may be a rude awakening to the child who has been sheltered from the world. He will not know what to make of the child who steals his lunch or calls him names. The school world is quite different from the home environment. Some of this shock can be softened if he has had nursery school even part time from age two on. You can answer his questions as they arise to make the adjustment to kindergarten easier. This is good learning for parents who need to learn objectivity. Children become masters at solving relationship problems, and they forgive and forget much faster than parents do. So stay as objective as you can.

Do start teaching how special he is and that handling the world situations in a loving way is the highest and the best. He does not have to act as others do to him to get what he wants.
God is working His purpose out through his blessed seed in his day-to-day world. With each challenge direct your child to solve problems with the highest and best for all concerned in mind.

If nursery school is not possible, schedule a time each day to play "school" at home. Lead it yourself, and occasionally ask a school age child in the neighborhood to play "school" with your child. Doing a neighborhood activity occasionally has merit. Taking your child to the zoo, the park, and other childrens" programs gives interesting subjects to write and tell and draw about. Read to and with your child on a daily basis. Make reading your focal point to learn about things, and your child will enjoy reading for life. Get information from your neighborhood school on what your child should be able to do on entering kindergarten and set a plan to accomplish that.

THE EARLY SCHOOL YEARS

Teacher, Teacher

REMEMBER: EVERY TEACHER HAS A GIFT TO GIVE EVERY STUDENT. It will not be the same for any two children. And every child has a gift to give his teacher. No two alike. If your child is having difficulty with his teacher, it may be that he is not accepting the gift. Being a teacher is a very high calling. Few teachers survive in teaching very long if their commitment and integrity are not strong enough.

REMEMBER: It is no accident that your child is in THAT teacher's classroom. Even though the principal tries to equate the classes, even if the parent tries to manipulate the placement, or the teacher tries to request a favorite student, in the end THERE ARE NO ACCIDENTS. The reason may not be clear to any of the parties concerned. The gift to be given is important to the life setting of that child.

Each teacher has mastered these important traits or will review as a necessity: self-determination, organization, self-discipline, patience, understanding, impartiality and goal setting. Teachers must know themselves very well before they step one foot into the classroom. A high level of morality, values, unconditioned love, forgiveness and generosity are required of the individualized spirit who is called "teacher". Every teacher is inspired, desires the best for his pupils and will loyally defend them or extend himself beyond what is required. He will go the extra mile for the good of the child or the class as a whole. That is the commitment I have seen over and over with every teacher I have been acquainted with over the years.

It is not without reason that the teacher has been honored through out history. Why, then, does it not seem to be so today in this country? The honor previously was a "false" honor, in that few were able to read or write so anyone who could, was honored. Today, with education more prevalent reading and writing is more or less taken for granted, so are the teachers. This too will pass. We do not presume that teachers are saints and have nothing to learn in this lifetime. Not at all. Some teachers are philanderers, alcoholics, and some drug addicts. But not as many as would be found in the general population. They are a product of their time. The teachers being prepared today are of the highest quality and will be a blessing to the profession. I expect to see them honored more and more for their worthy calling.

HELP YOUR CHILD GET THE MOST OUT OF SCHOOL

Assume first of all that the school is not his only form of education, that YOU are his teacher! Prepare yourself to be so.

First, be up to date on the important subjects to be studied each year. Plan educational trips to museums, art galleries, the planetarium and a real farm to expand upon his knowledge of the world around him.

Second, plan lessons based on the published curriculum for the grade level and provide one-to-one time to study in depth. A child who has some background in a subject will get so much more out of the study when it's presented at school.

Third, plan and insist on a daily study period emphasizing reading, writing and arithmetic.

Fourth, send a rested, well-fed,(a good breakfast included) healthy and happy child to school, daily. The benefits will be noticeable. Studies show that success in school depends on these four most important criteria. Providing a structured life away from school has merit. A regular bed time and meal times, make for a more secure, rested child.

Provide music lessons and membership in scouting-like organizations. But most of all, provide the religious training that your child will need to fulfill his high purposes in this life. Do not lose sight of your contract with this child as the years go by, Provide whatever you promised to prepare him to be whether it be a musician, an artist, an architect, or a minister.Recognize the Spiritual awakening within him and encourage it by sharing your own experiences in Spirit. Regularly; allow time for sharing mutual ideas and realizations.

Do not be in a great hurry to start your child in kindergarten or to rush him through school. Take note if the teacher says your child doesn't listen well, doesn't follow directions, has difficulty getting along with others, needs extra attention, has problems making his letters, coloring, hearing sounds or identifying the
letters being taught. Especially take notice if he has a late birthday. Just a few of these things are indications that another year to grow up would be beneficial. Also, have your child thoroughly screened by a doctor. Many children get far along in school before a hearing or sight problem is discovered. When it is discovered, do something about it. Some parents believe that their child's social development will be impaired because of a stigma attached to glasses, hearing aids and /or medication for hyperactivity. All the while the child suffers from not seeing accurately or hearing precisely or not being able to settle down long enough to learn. We need to be willing to provide the tools to make his learning a complete success. Glasses and hearing aids are willingly provided by service organizations free, to needy children. It has always been a mystery to me why certain parents

whose child needs them desperately refuse to accept them.

There is no time table that requires a child to finish high school at seventeen. An extra year in any grade will be a benefit in the long run if the child is of normal intelligence, but working below grade level. In many schools the decision is left entirely up to the parents. Find out if this is true in your child's case and keep him back a year if necessary. Do what is best for your child disregarding the system. Feeling that "I'm always behind. I don't know what is going on in my classroom," is daily failure and instrumental in lowering self-esteem."Everybody else is ahead of me." is a terrible feeling and no one should feel that way for long.

Extra homework is never the answer. A home study course to supplement the school program is the answer. If the parent can't devote the time or patience, if you come to loggerheads every time you try to help, then a tutor needs to be hired. Remember the school provides only part of the child's education. Six hours a day for ten months does not ensure a complete education. The rest is up to the parent.

It is important that a balance be kept in a child's life. If academic work is difficult, provide something that he can do to be successful. Find out his talent- drama, gymnastics, swimming, whatever it is- and encourage it.Something he can excel in will keep the balance. One grandfather took his grandson into his shop and taught him to turn wooden bowls on his lathe. He shared his hobby with him. The grandson won several prizes at the county fair. This balanced out his difficultly at school.

I challenge you to get involved with the school and the programs. Be informed. Overcome any leftover antagonisms and get involved. Volunteer in your child's classroom, or if that isn't possible, the school library. Many schools welcome parental assistance,when it is regular and can be depended upon. School is definitely a day-to-day thing. Teachers plan programs in advance and schedules are adhered to daily.
Be a dependable volunteer.

I notice a lack of understanding by many parents in encouraging regular attendance on the part of their children. Some of the excuses are, "We stayed up too late last night," or "We're going out of town so Mike has to stay with his grandma in another city." School doesn't come first anymore. Of course, the school doesn't want sick children, but if a child is absent more than fifteen days in a year without seeing a doctor about it, something is wrong.

Habitual absence and tardiness cause a child to get a wrong view of life and he will be absent or late for work as an adult. The child who is never there on Monday because that's his mother's day off is learning a very bad habit and is being educationally short changed.

HOW TO HELP AN INATTENTIVE CHILD

If the report comes to you from your child's teacher, or you observe it yourself, that your child has difficulty staying with a task (hypnotized by TV doesn't count), is confused or non-responsive, it is a sign that your child needs direction and help.

First, clarify in your mind exactly what is expected at school. Support your child by getting suggestions from his teacher. Follow through. Doing excellent work under your tutelage will build confidence and show his possibilities to his teacher. This well may get him off center and reveal to him his greater abilities and encourage him to set higher standards for himself. In addition, a certain comradeship may develop: We can lick this problem together. Very often children feel so overwhelmed by the school's expectations that they withdraw in confusion. Teachers try by explaining repeatedly. This sometimes results in more trauma on the student's part and he may hide the problem from his parents for years. A simple request, "Ask for help at home," by the teacher may send the child reeling with fear. Feelings of self are very tender in this regard and so long lasting that some people spend their whole lifetime believing that they can't do and school is hard. THE PARENT IS THE TEACHER, TOO. Don't delegate it all to the school.

The second step is building up the self from within. Quiet time one-to-one is so valuable in releasing fear, frustration, confusion and restoring faith, confidence, determination and goal setting. If the question is school work; lift the child's view by acknowledging that within everyone are the answers to every question. A clear plan, a way to go is always available to the child when he clears his mind of all limiting thoughts and allows God's solution, God's answer, God's plan to come forth through his own mind. Teach the child positive mind-clearing affirmations like "God is my help in every need." Say to your child, "When you are confused, feel helpless or don't understand, say to yourself, God knows how to do this and I know how to do this. Then try again." Say it over and over until he automatically responds in this manner.

The third step is practicing at home by visualization of what is expected in class. Visualization is a powerful tool that can be learned easily at an early age. Practice in the evening what is desired to occur at school the next day. Expecting a good successful outcome because the math work is done and the spelling words learned, makes for a confident child.

If sports figures can make a noticeable improvement in their game by visualizing every move ahead of time, why can't children do the same? Visit your child's classroom and observe the routine so that you can bring to the practice visualization sessions authentic situations and chronicle of events to your child's mind
.
If inattention is the problem at school, together practice visualizing him sitting quietly, reading his assignment, doing his math in the time allowed and being finished when the teacher asks for the work. If he claims that others are bothering him or that the class is too noisy to work, do the same visualization but make suggestions that his concentration is so great

that he is not disturbed by others.

Spend some time in visualization feeling good about the successfully accomplished work. A visualization session could go as follows:

"Dear, when I visited your classroom today, I noticed that your math class came right after recess. Everyone came in, sat down and went to work on the page listed on the board. Let's visualize your classroom together. You come in, sit down and take out your book. Instead of looking around the room a bit, you look on the board and find your math assignment right away. Your pencil is already sharp and you have the paper you need, so you begin. You know exactly how to do the problems. You write them down quickly and work the problems without looking up at all. You are confident that they are right, and they are! What a good feeling to have the work done on time when your teacher asks for it and to get 100%, besides. You feel great about yourself! Now, open your eyes and feel glad about yourself."

The fourth, most important part:The parents understanding must grow too in order to support the child from the problem to the solution. Instill the positive attitude into the child's mind and give him a method of problem solving that will stay with him for a lifetime in his subconsciousness mind. The parent needs to study, take classes and use the Spiritual Mind Treatment himself and be a graphic example in solving life's problems. Sharing how you have overcome similar problems is often helpful when it is of the highest level.

The fifth, and most important plan is to listen. If the problem is in the area of relationships, listen and learn. Adults and children too often do not represent situations accurately when they are too close to them. If your child is being the victim, careful listening is in order. As much as we love and trust our child, a true picture of the situation may not be revealed. The belief that another child is keeping him from doing his work is quite common. By past experience I have noticed that any diversion from the task is welcome by an inattentive child. Also, a child who really doesn't want to be disturbed, won't be, no matter what the situation is or who his neighbors are. Frequently, the child sitting across the room is the one who is accused of interrupting him.

Children are human, too. If they are looking for a problem, they'll find it. If they are looking for an excuse, they'll find that, too. Water seeks its own level. Two hyperactive kids will find each other like magic.

The sixth method of solving problems we all teach but need to be reminded of from time to time: thoughtfulness and good manners. A quick "I'm sorry," when accidentally smacking someone across the head with the tetherball will usually avoid a fight. If the parent notices that his child has difficulty getting along with others, always wanting his own way, not caring about the feelings of others, a bit of role playing is helpful. You play him and let him play the other fellow. Then reverse the action and let him explore a better way to solve the problem. Sometimes children get in a habit of handling situations the same way every time without thought.

The old adage"To get a friend you have to be a friend" is the Law of Cause and Effect. You get back exactly what you give. On the highest level, God is equally present in everyone at all times. Looking for that God in others will bring permanent peaceful relationships. Instruct your child to find the good in everyone and sometimes naming the good qualities in that person will lift the thought and action.

Remember to always look for the good in each situation presented to your child and the valuable lesson will become a milestone instead of a stumbling block.

"The greatest gift to life is to learn to love yourself."
Alyce Soden

Chapter 8

GOAL: Being a Fountain of Love

The greatest most important goal of all is to learn to express love to every person everywhere and all the time. In order to do this one must love themselves first.

Children come into this world loving themselves and accepting themselves very well. We as parents and family introduce the other ideas such as you're not good, you're not behaving, you're not doing like someone else did at this age. Gradually, that good self whom we loved on entering this life is eroded by judging, and should's, no's and stop that's.

To counter balance the mental attitude that begins to develop feelings of being less than or not good enough, parents need to consciously daily remind this beautiful child of who he is and why he's here which is to love himself first, love others second and to act in love at all times.

How important is recognizing the loving nature in a child? It is important that he love himself first. Repeatedly we have rewarded the elder child when he expresses love to the younger child instead of jealousy and it is important that he be reassured that he can love himself also.

When the theme of the home is love and respect

for every member of the family, a child can grow within that love and will express it greatly. Parents need to be alert to the signs of not enough love which are: not expressing love in daily family exchanges.

When a person feels out of love with themselves they often feel as if they cannot spare any love for others and act in a manner that expresses that attitude.

When a person feels full of love for themselves they appear to have enough and to spare for others.

We have been taught that loving ones self was bad. Loving others was good. This comes from a misinterpretation of the Biblical passage:" (Matthew 19:19) Love thy neighbor as thyself. If one cannot love themselves, they will never be able to love their neighbor.

It also comes from the idea that there is a limited amount of love to go around. And that we must keep that small amount we have been given for ourselves.

People get very strange ideas when they feel a lack of love. A lady I met felt she could only have one friend and that friend should not have any other friends. She was really feeling a lack of love.

In counseling a mother who had two children, she confided in me that she could not love her second child as she had so little love she must give it all to her first child.

We tend to express our self-esteem (how we feel about ourselves) in our dealings with others from our fullness of love or lack of love feelings. The greatest gift to life is to love yourself.

There is no lack of love. Love is the energy that God broadcasts to this earth, throughout all space and time. There can never be a shortage of love. As we learn to tap into that endless source through meditation and prayer we become love filled and blessed. We discover there is no end to love and any idea of a shortage evaporates.

I challenge you to discover for yourself this blessing of love. How great it is. We are basking in it, breathing it, living in it at all times. We only have to allow it's entrance into our being and we are connected to this endless supply. When we discover for ourselves the fullness of love, we can act from this fullness allowing greater love to flow into ourselves and out to our families, friends, acquaintances, then the world. We have enough and to spare.

Use this visualization yourself. Let your children participate:

Sit quietly in the sunlight. Feel the rays of light on your shoulders. Visualize that that warmth is the love of God flowing to you and through you warming you to the very center of your being. See yourself filled with that love until you are full to the brim. Let that love overflow to each person in your family one after the other until they are filled. Then let that love pour out to your neighbors, your classmates and anyone who comes to your mind. Fill the world with love.

On returning to yourself, notice that you are still centered in God's love and filled full. There is no lack nor can there ever be. Love is the energy of God.

LEARNING TO USE THE POWER OF LOVE

Using the power of Love to heal relationships is a very important step in developing a positive self-esteem and higher level of consciousness. Learning to love yourself and allow that God loves you also to the greatest degree brings about a confidence in one's self. When one feels completely loved, giving love unconditioned to others is almost automatic. When you discover that you don't have to keep your guard up all the time you will automatically treat everyone faithfully with love. Your self-esteem will grow and expand until you truly hold yourself in high esteem.

Some people do not feel loved or lovable or for various reasons are not able to give love. So allow your mind and heart to be so filled with love for yourself that your overflow goes out to others you may meet.

It is sad to say some people have never experienced love, unconditioned love in this life time and/or before. When this is the case there tends to be skepticism about it or any person who expresses love. Under the guise that children need to learn what life's all about, love may be withheld from an early age. How sad this is. When no knowledge of love is the case, disbelief goes along with it. However, Spirit does not allow us to stand still. You may be the instrument to teach this person unconditional love. This takes patience as there are many more evidences for withholding love, if you are looking for them than for love given freely without strings, unconditionally.

Children and adults can visualize the plenteous love of God as they stand in the shower letting the water flow over them, cleansing the limiting thoughts and opening themselves to the great love of the Universe that is restoring and renewing the bounteous love God is always providing.

The goal of being the fountain of love in the human family is worthy of each emerging soul.

Learning the meaning of these affirmations and acting as if they are so will set one well along the way to reach this goal:

God's love fills my mind, heart, body and world.

I do not exclude anyone or anything.

My love warms and brightens every part of my life and
   the life of everyone who crosses my path.

Every thought, word and deed are expressed by loving
   myself and everyone else in this world.

I am love in expression.

I am love.

USING LOVE TO HEAL RELATIONSHIPS

Situation: The neighborhood children are not getting along well, causing great unhappiness.
Goal to be set: Happy, friendly children playing together harmoniously.

Plan 1: Pray about it daily, both parent and child. Love and bless each child with God's love. Know this is successful and look for signs that it is working. Participate WITH your child in all areas.

Plan 2: Devise a plan to express love to each child individually. Ask one at a time over to play.

Plan 3: When harmonious play is achieved add another participant when you can be present to begin it. Be sure not to exclude anyone in the neighborhood.

Plan 4: Hold an idea session after each play period with your child to find more ways to creatively share love with each person.

Plan 5: Learning that happy relationships are not accidents, but a plan working or worked out in the mind of one or more of the participants is an invaluable lesson for life.

Plan 6: Set out to prove the power of love to enhance the child's self-esteem and change the quality of relationships.

Parents may believe that THEY must do the planning and executing of activities leading to a harmonious end. Include your child and see insightful changes revealed.

DON'T FORGET TO RECORD YOUR ACTIONS AND PROGRESS. DON'T GIVE UP!

As children learn to use goal setting, visualization and affirmations, they will respond in a more confident manner to challenges in school, and a camaraderie will develop between parent and child. Start small. Don't try to eat the whole elephant at one time. Perfect the plan and build confidence as you go. As William Arthur Ward said, "A success in life is someone who worked. A failure in life is one who wished." With practice the child will begin asking to set a goal in an area of need because he knows IT WORKS!

Children who do not feel good about themselves often complain that others are calling them 'snobbish' or ' uppity.' Her mother asked for help with such a problem. The girl was a seven year old enlightened child.

What do you do on a rainy afternoon with no toys in the house to entertain a four and seven year old? Get out the drawing paper and crayons. The girls dove right in. I drew a large circle which came out quite well, I thought. But I didn't know what to do next, so I just waited. In the course of the conversation, I asked the older girl why she was here in this life, now. Her answer was "to live ". "Very good!" Then I drew wavy lines all around my circle. The wavy lines represent other children like your classmates, I explained. "They do not see you as you truly are. They are confused and do not know what to make of your calmness, peacefulness and knowing what you want to do and be, but you know who your are." Then I put a line in the circle and finished the word. "You are here for a special purpose.You are here..." " to LOVE." She exclaimed. Sometimes an illustrated talk can be most effective.

RULE: When outside pressures seem overwhelming, return to your greatest self. Lift your eyes and see your true divinity. LOVE, always love yourself!

Illustration #1 You are LOVE!

RAISE HIM UP IN THE WAY HE SHOULD GO AND HE'LL NOT DEPART FROM IT.

Raise your child with love and he'll not depart from it. He will find love everywhere he goes and give love in return. Being a fountain of love brings back blessing after blessing. This is the greatest gift a parent can ever give.

Find an opportunity to visualize being a fountain of love. Some public buildings have fountains. Look for pictures or better still find a fountain. Sit where you can inhale the exhilarating spray and see the rainbow of glistening water. Point out how peaceful and comforting it is to sit and enjoy this beautiful place. Use the moment to instill a mental picture within both you and your child. You can bring again in your mind at any time.

Being a fountain of love exercise:
Recall from your memory the fountain, the water, the picture. Open up your senses to feel the air, the sounds, the rushing water. Remember how it felt as the wind gently sent the spray over you. Remember the rainbows and the glistening droplets.

When the mind is filled with the memory of the fountain reveal that the water is like God's love flowing endlessly and the fountain is like yourself and your child being that which allows God's love to flow. Fill your mind with this exquisitely beautiful experience.

When we provide experiences like this for our children we pave the way for them to fulfill their life's goal: Being a fountain of love.

"Within every right desire is the power of its fulfillment. All desire, directed by the God within, goes forth with the feeling of love and blesses always." Saint Germain.

"Life is a blackboard upon which we consciously or unconsciously write those messages which govern us.

E..Holmes

Chapter 9

GOAL SETTING

Every person in life should have a goal or many goals and work toward them until completed and then get started on another. It is true that goal setting is not a common procedure held to by people in general. But people who are doers and successful are people with a purpose. People who accomplish things in life do not let the happenings of life direct them. THEY DIRECT THEIR LIVES.

The attitude "whatever will be, will be" does not build bridges or further mans development on any plane of existence. If you went about life without a plan and still arrived at a very successful place, good for you. Most of the world has not found this method successful. Those who are successful have a PLAN.

What about the parent who sets goals for his child from early age? "My son is going to be a professional ball player.""My daughter is going to sing at the Met." Is that so bad? Does it really limit the child's freedom of choice? I am a strong believer that a high and lofty goal is certainly better than no goal at all. Let's look at the father who desires that his son be a ball player. He will probably spend much time with him, teaching him to throw, catch, run and hit the ball. He will also help him with his homework so that his grades will be good enough to play ball. Is that bad? Not at all. With his father's attention, that boy will go far in anything he decides later to do.

What about the girl who is being trained to sing at the Met? That means music lessons, taking her to concerts and operas. She will need to broaden her education in the classics. Training how to move about gracefully requires dancing lessons or modeling lessons. Learning to speak and sing develops poise and self confidence. These must be provided by the parents. All in all, every child can become a hybrid tea rose or a wild rose depending on the parent's interest and willingness to provide the opportunities needed.

As you can see, I am a strong believer that a high and lofty goal is certainly better than no goal at all. The child will go farther with his goal if the parent's complete interest and attention is on him to study hard to be a doctor than if the parent shrugs and says, "You choose what you want to be when it's time." It has been my experience that a child goes farther more easily when he knows "what and why" at an early age.

The best way I know to make this come about is for the parents to start out setting goals and, as soon as the child is old enough to set his own goals, teach him how important it is and help him reach them.

The parent needs to make the "big goal" for the child's life and find little goals, short term goals for the child to accomplish. The child who didn't participate (dropped out) of the dance recital last year mostly because she wasn't mature enough to participate needs to try again this year. Learning to set long-term goals and short-term goals is a very important life trait.

You may wonder what kind of goal you could set as a new parent for this tiny bundle that only seems interested in the basics of life. Search your mind, your abilities, your interests and your experiences in life. Why would a child pick you for a parent? Perhaps it is to learn something specific. Do you play the piano, or are you an artist, like to build things, understand and participate in government? History is filled with children who followed in their parents' footsteps. So what is special about you?

What kind of life do you want for your child? The kind you have had? Good question. How can you prepare your child for a life better than yours? By setting goals and teaching him to set goals. By giving him the training and experiences far beyond what is given in school and sharing your talents and interests with him.

You can also have his purpose revealed to you in dreams or visions by asking over and over until the answer comes.

You may ask, "Won't that make a warped child, always trying to live up to a parent's dream?" Perhaps, and he may hate you for it. But he will probably go through that"hate parents stage" anyway. Any time or money spent is sure to benefit him in some way you do not know at the time and will certainly make a more confident, secure child if he's encouraged and praised along the way.

Start simple and make short range goals like: learn to play that piano piece in two weeks. Finish writing that paper for school in one week. Finish digging the weeds out of the garden, turn over the soil and plant in two weeks. Notice, the word FINISH was used. Children need to learn the internal reward for completion, the job well done and learn to make the commitment to do whatever it takes to complete the task. What a boon to self-esteem. I can do it. I am doing it. I have done it! No other reward is necessary. This develops reasons for self-love. Goals can be set and plans made, but if no effort is given to doing the work needed, all will be to no avail. Finishing is as important as starting in developing a positive view of himself.

If your child dawdles or avoids finishing things, take the time to remind him of the numerous activities he has completed and how great he felt about himself when he did. Make a list and keep adding to that list. Let it be called I'm Loving Myself When I Finish List.

What about rewards? He can get all bound up in getting $5.00 for all the 'A's on his report card and miss what's important to learn from the class. A job well done is reward in itself, increases self-esteem and feels good, if the parents celebrate it..

The Plan for Setting Goals is simple: First, parent and child need to combine their efforts and set a goal. Choose an appropriate goal for the age and interest of the child.

Second, plan what action is needed to reach that goal, both parent and child participating (set a time limit if appropriate)

Third: record the actions taken and the results along the way.

Fourth: celebrate together when the goal is reached. If for some reason the goal is not reached in a reasonable time, renegotiate the plan to a more workable means and proceed again. The important part is reaching the goal.
For example: The report card comes home indicating that the child is deficient in spelling. Parent and child discuss the matter (calmly and logically). Together they arrive at what the matter is and set a goal:" to spell well and get 100% on tests at school next quarter."

Plan of action: Child will spend 20 minutes each day studying the words immediately after dinner. The parent will give the test daily to see the progress made.

If this plan of action is acceptable, both sign the goal contract. If the child does this without reminder daily, great! If he does not, add that to the contract. Keep record of the parents tests during the week and the school tests when they come in.

Be willing to renegotiate or rewrite the plan as you work with it to see that it fits the situation.

Celebrate the goal reached when the next report

card comes home with good grades in spelling.

REMEMBER; both parent and child must participate in the action part of this plan. You cannot send him to his room to do it all by himself. So write a part for yourself into the plan and endeavor to fulfill it.

LIFE DIRECTION GOALS (AGES 7-8-9)

There is nothing that children like to do better than talk about what they want to do, be or have when they grow up. Children get ideas of what they want their life to be starting at an early age. Of course, it may change many times as their interests change, but that is to be expected. Astute attention on the part of the parent will unearth a general direction or underlying idea. If the parent and child have worked together solving problems using the aforementioned plan, the groundwork will already be laid to build a broad base of confidence.

When the parent asks the child what he wants to be when he grows up, the natural answer will be the profession or kind of work the child has been interested in lately. And that is a good beginning. Parent and child can explore together what that particular calling requires in special abilities, training, personality traits, and education. List the rewards, kind of life style and other benefits as you discover them.

The information they do not have can be researched in the local library. Get acquainted with someone who does that kind of work and ask questions. Really investigate. The kind of life that profession will provide is interesting to explore. When a thirteen-year-old boy was most interested in a career in the Navy, he had the opportunity to visit a relative who was career Navy and his family. He toured the base and a ship and generally got the feel of that kind of life. It wasn't long before he was exploring something else. That kind of life was glamorous in some ways and not for him in others. Meanwhile, he learned a great deal about himself, his vision in life and how to match it up with a lifetime career.

With technology advancing as fast as it is it may seem difficult to prepare your child for his future life work. Of course there will always be people serving professions and preparation in those fields have not changed over the years. Doctors, lawyers, politicians and teachers need many years of college education. Computer technology has added new fields to the colleges, Generally, give him a well rounded education in all fields. He will find his way.

A few of the aspects of life natural to a particular profession to be reviewed are: life style, education, special abilities and aptitudes matched to overall life commitment, purpose for this life, serving God to the greatest degree.

Of course, we know that we can, and are expected to serve God to the highest degree wherever we find ourselves, but some incarnating souls have a more specific commitment.

When the goal is set (this can happen at any age) devise a plan to follow. What courses need to be taken in school. What if any skills need to be mastered, or further study provided by parents. A well prepared person goes farther that one who just falls into the job.

<u>Be Prepared.</u> Preparation is what school is all about and a life well prepared for is a greater more successful life.

What happens if the youngster starts but never finishes the lofty goal you as parent set for him? Nothing is ever lost. All will be used in some way. Certainly, a person who studies to be a doctor and ends up a pharmaceutical salesman is not lost. He uses much of his training still. In my view, the more education a person gets, the better prepared for life he will be. Goal setting encourages one to stay in school to reach his desired goal.

PREPARATION FOR A SUCCESSFUL LIFE

A welfare mother couldn't afford to give her nine-year-old son the kind of vacation she wished, and he wanted something special that summer. She had a friend living near the campus of Stanford University who would let them roll out their sleeping bags on the floor of her apartment for a few days. With borrowed bicycles they toured the campus and even ate in the campus cafeteria. Where do you think that boy will want to go when college time rolls around?

When we provide experiences like this for our

children we pave the way for them to incorporate the idea into their life plans.

It is sad that going to church is such an unfashionable activity and Sunday School is not considered a necessity by our parents of today. I see how children react. They thirst after lessons of the Spirit and learning how to master and direct their lives. Parents who include Sunday School in their over all picture of priorities for their children are giving them the greatest possible gift.

The Jewish mother who demanded that her son be a doctor or the Irish Catholic mother who dedicated her son to the church to be a priest at an early age believed firmly that "If you raise him up in the way that he should go, he will not depart from it."

"What would it be like to be born into Heaven? I believe our babies do not know that they are not being born into heaven. They are given a vehicle (body) that serves them well when they master it, someone to greet them and care for them, as well as other preparation. How can we create Heaven on earth into which all our children are born?"   *Alyce Soden*

CHAPTER 10

LEVELS OF SOUL DEVELOPMENT

You may ask why babies are born with defective bodies, a disease or limited minds. It is not at all they were born in sin or that their parents had sinned. The physical body is governed by the Laws of Nature. The soul is governed by Spiritual Law. If the mother or father has a disease such as AIDS that can be passed to the developing fetus, then it will (following nature's law) be diseased unless interceded. The child seems to be the innocent victim. Not so.

The soul residing in that body has contracted to experience that limitation prior to birth for a number of reasons. It may be to develop greater sensitivity for others so afflicted or limited and it may experience this type of limitation for many lifetimes until the lesson is learned. The signal that the lesson is learned is when the soul overcomes the defective instrument in many ways and returns to a normal unrestricted life. Such souls are also our teachers.

Another reason for choosing or creating a defective body may be to bring a message to the world or perform some important mission.

Souls, generally, can be classed by their level of understanding and use of Universal Law.

First, the young soul, or earth-bound, desires to return almost immediately to the earth plane and will accept even a limited life or a handicapped life to accomplish this desire. Gradually, this soul will overcome the physical handicap and will evolve to the next level where greater choice is desired and available. This is not to imply that all handicapped persons are of the lower level of soul development. They may be of a much higher level of soul development but have chosen to occupy the defective instrument for certain gifts to be given, or as a special opportunity through a parental association that was deemed beneficial.

A dear colleague of mine had polio at an early age and was severely handicapped. Because of this he studied and became a teacher. A more loving and inspired teacher you could not find. His devoted students forgot about his handicap and returned his love. He demonstrated his high level of soul on a daily basis in his classroom.

The young soul is usually quite affected by race consciousness (the beliefs of the world) and is often headstrong to experience every negative and harmful addictive opportunity that comes along. Leaving this level, a person begins to "get his life together" know what he wants and how to go about getting it. Others seem to float about with the wind no matter the fine example shown by parents and friends. Inner direction or lack of it are easily discerned in young children.

Second, the next higher level of attainment or soul development allows the soul to view the Akashic record for the purpose of evaluating past life experiences and for planning for optimum growth in the next incarnation. Some life choices provide a slow steady progress, others more accelerated. The individualization at this level of soul may choose to have his chosen pattern or life plan imprinted in his consciousness as in his conscience by which the soul will match and judge the progress being made toward his afore chosen goal. Freedom of choice is the basis for this level of soul.

Inherent in this level is the right to choose not to incarnate at all, or the length or quality of the incarnation. This explains the stillborn. The soul decides, on reviewing the records, that this life is not suited to his needs after all, and he releases the reservation for that instrument. There may be time before birth that another soul may choose that life, but sometimes it's too late and no one chooses, so the instrument dies.

It is said there is a shortage of mother's wombs of sufficient enlightenment for all the advanced souls who wish to incarnate at any one time .
The souls may have to wait or reserve their place for another time or take a lesser life while waiting.

Every life is important however inconsequential it may seem. Some lives provide more soul growth than do others.

The third level of soul has passed through the

first two and seeks to serve man and God. A soul in this level contracts and prepares to teach, give succor, and generally bind up the wounds, feed the hungry, shelter and protect the weak, the young and the aged. This level is not self serving but generously giving of self completely. A soul may be deeply religious in this level, which indicates preparedness for the next level.

Being many faceted individuals, it needs to be said that each life experience tends to be at the soul level. Many may still carry an addiction, negative personality traits or a life style choice along through several life times before releasing it.

The level of the Light Worker, totally committed to God, is expected to have mastered all lesser levels. The purpose of this soul level is to be a way-shower for God's purpose on earth. This soul is not as attached to the earth life and frequently chooses the purpose of the assignment. This soul spends time between incarnations preparing the skills needed to perform the task committed to his care on earth. The gifted writer, artist, musician, scientist, or mathematician have mastered much in each level.

Preparation between lifetimes becomes more extensive at each level and may be revealed at an earlier age of life. This explains why great souls like Mozart, Bach and Beethoven revealed their greatness at such an early age and their subsequent life followed an inner pattern of much to accomplish in that lifetime. Memory of former lives or training on the other side beyond the veil is rare.

Every life on this side is important, however inconsequential it may seem. Some lives provide more soul growth than others.

No soul goes through life without Guides living concurrently with themselves and Master Guides on the other side as inner advisors. The Spirit level of the Master Guides increases as the soul evolves. Competent guides are always available.

Some Master Guides on the other side choose to accept assignments occasionally to further man kinds development in their area of expertise. Some are still well known in recent history. I am reminded the story of Saint Germain who's responsibility it was to inspire the greatest possible Constitution for the fledgling thirteen colonies. Jefferson's proposed constitution had been debated and debated. Each and every word had been examined. Now was the time to ratify it. Every man knew that he would be marked as an enemy of the king. By signing this document it might be his death warrant. It was a tense moment when president pro tem, George Washington called for the the question. Not a sound was heard. He called again. Not a sound.
Finally, on the third call a voice was heard, saying,"Question." And the vote was begun. No one to this day knows who called for the question. It is said that Saint Germain, in his eagerness to bring ratification overstepped his boundaries and called for the question.
.
Old souls have served as Master Guides and are

easily noted by their non-judgmental attitudes and patience toward others. They have experienced and overcome many limitations. They understand the purpose of life. Their motto might be "there but for the grace of God go I." And in most cases they have experienced that limitation in some previous lifetime, eventually overcoming it. Temptations still come to them as an echo of a former experience. Souls who are afflicted or living lives of addictions may at any time cast them aside, as they are limiting and non-productive, and dead ended. Those consciously in the search for enlightenment will find solis that once an addiction is overcome one need never experience that limitation again.

The end goal for all souls is oneness with God. All are on that pathway, learning, growing, overcoming; falling back to relearn lessons, all are still on the pathway. Being gentle with one's self and loving one's self in spite of imperfections is a definite plus. Being non-judgmental with one's self and others is an important trait to cultivate.

Let's return to the beginning premise: <u>the fetus is governed by Natural Law, the soul by Spiritual Law.</u> The number of lifetimes is not important. The level of attainment and lessons learned is important. "Freedom of choice is the birthright of every living soul." Ernest Holmes. Before and during an incarnation and eternally, there is no timetable. Life will continue until all have reached the level of the Christ. As it is said of old, "The ox is slow but the carth is patient."

"Everything that opposes harmony and spontaneous unity will prove disastrous to the child's health, sooner or later." Ernest Holmes

Chapter 11

ON HEALING YOUR CHILD

Scientific Prayer holds great power to heal the child who desires to remain in his present life. Using this method to replace negative subjective impressions with positive life enhancing impressions heals the child's physical body and physical world. Children have amazing recuperative power. They can be running a life-threatening temperature one minute and be playing happily the next.

For long term healing, free from recurring illness, the family needs to be the focal point of the Treatment. Long-held attitudes and beliefs by the parents that little children are usually sick or are easily infected by childhood diseases need to be addressed."Playing with a child who has chicken pox is a sure way for your little one to get it." Not always!

The childs' mental attitude about disease is often patterned after his parent's belief such as: I'm not a well person. I must be careful. I must not get cold, so I can't play in the snow. These are life-long positive or negative impressions being formed. Many physical ailments disappear as the child matures such as: allergies to food, drugs, feathers, wool or fur. Yet the parent may still closely guard that child from those threats to his health. You know you can't (have that, do

that or be that) because of_____.
You fill in the blank. Some parents are dependent on certain drugs for a cure when a good healthy diet would have prevented the problem. The body will heal itself and does automatically.

Early impressions of poor health leave lasting limitations in the subjective mind if not consciously changed, will need to be overcome in later life.

Parents need to examine their beliefs about health as regarding their child especially if a recurring disease is the experience. The question might be asked:"What am I thinking, saying or doing that Johnnie's asthma is the result?"

A worried mother came asking for healing her child of his recurring asthma. The practitioner listened to the mother's concerns and did a treatment for the situation. This occurred again and again. Several weeks passed with no visible change. One day the practitioner had a reason to visit in the home. As the mother and practitioner were discussing other business, the child did something the mother was distressed about. The mother shouted out,"God will punish you for that." The child appeared to cower at those words and quietly left the room.

The practitioner asked, " Do you threaten God's punishment often?" The mother was taken aback as if she had not heard herself. Then quietly she said, "My mother used to say that to me." The practitioner suggested she say, "God loves you!" instead. The child's asthma dissipated.

How often did we say as a child that we would not treat our children "that way" as our parents had just treated us. We pass on poor methods to the next generation unconsciously. Pay attention, read, be open-minded, and try new ideas. Many methods are worthy and self esteem building, others are not. Your words have power and affect your child in some way. Consciously keep your thoughts, words and deeds in heaven when dealing with your child.

Disease of the body is an effect. Discovering the cause is a sure way to heal the body permanently. Sometimes in this fast world illness is a cry to slow down and pay attention to me.

Every child is perfect in God's eyes. There is not now or ever has been a sick child. As we learn to see more and more through the perfect vision of the One, it becomes a reality for ourselves and our children. And from this point of view, we parents or the world cannot make a sick child.

The clear-eyed view that God's love and grace, guidance and protection are always surrounding each family member provides a Power that relieves parents' guilt and allows them to let the highest and best be the result,which is a perfect -functioning body.

What would it be like to be born into the Kingdom of Heaven? What kind of life would that be? It certainly would include being loved unconditionally, being secure, cared for and trusted. It would be a place where even the unsteady legs of the toddler would be safe, protected, loved and regarded as perfect. It is my belief that our babies do not know that they are not being born into Heaven. Their needs for a loving, safe, and accepting environment continue after birth. What a challenge and an opportunity to make this kind of life true for every child.

HEAL THE CAUSE AND THE EFFECT WILL DISAPPEAR

Easier said than done to even find the cause! If you have sought the cause out there in the world to no avail, look closer to home. Look within yourself. Listen to what you are saying about yourself, the world and especially your child. If you feel you must struggle with life to make ends meet, or compromise your principles to keep your life together or any other false impression that parents may carry home with them, drop them before you enter your door. Just like the dirt on your feet, you bring home the trauma of the world, and your little one, especially if he's watching TV, will have a great number of negative impressions within himself.
All that he sees, feels and experiences make up his impression of what life is all about.

How do you change your view of life and your child's, also? MEDITATION! Time in the silence will change your life experience, heal any sickness that appears in your family and change the cause from negative to positive.

Begin with the premise that all physical bodies are created by God and every person is an individualization of God, an avenue for God to express to the greatest degree. Everything was made by God out of God so no thing in the world-be it grasses, trees, drugs, people or any other thing-can harm you or your child. Then hold that precious child of yours as if you are God holding him and blessing him with all the love and tenderness you can give.

Do you remember the touch of your mother's hand? or perhaps your father's hand? Does it have a soothing, reassuring feeling that all is well? Somehow, you are safe from the threats generated in the world. Touch your child. Give him that security that is not available in any other way, from anyone else but you.

We do not wish to give the impression that modern medicine should be avoided. Wonderful advancements are being made all the time. Remember these advancements as well as the doctors who provide them are of God, also.

Doctors have been known to rise far above their knowledge at the time to heal a sick child. Demand and expect the best care in every instance. Work with your physician in prayer and meditation. Prayer has been proved to make a difference. So do it!

In an emergency, UNTIL THE DOCTOR COMES, or you can reach a doctor, a call to your Licensed Practitioner requesting Spiritual Mind Treatment. For a complete and permanent healing working with your minister to discover the cause will be helpful. The parent is usually the first one called when an accident or illness occurs. Parents have healing powers that will heal their child, as most children know. What do they do when they hurt themselves? They run to mother to kiss it well. This is not just imagination. It is the truth for the lifetime of that child and parent. So use it knowing that it really works.

What about laying on of hands? Great healing powers exude from the hands when you allow the energy to flow out of you. When you release it on a person who is sick or injured, it stabilizes the body systems and returns them to normal. It is not without reason to put one's hand on the forehead to feel the temperature. A healing energy goes out. So when you have a sick child, touch him, hold him and take him to the doctor for treatment.

Earaches are common problems with children. The parent can stop the pain and heal the infection by simply putting his cupped hand over the ear. If the neck muscles are also sore or swollen, put the finger over that area. The warmth and healing power of the parent's hand will alleviate the earache quickly. The child can do it for himself. If this method doesn't work or the problem reoccurs, take him to the doctor.

A psychic said, I never try to heal a child through the child. I always start through the parent. The parent has the natural power to heal any disease or injury a child may have. It's like a direct pipeline."

A fine, mature. seven-year- old boy was having difficulty settling down in school. He was a top student but spent more and more time socializing and less and less in preparing his lessons. Asking about his family, the teacher discovered that his mother was pregnant with her third child. It was a difficult pregnancy; she had been ill and nearly lost the baby. Now her life was in jeopardy. No wonder the boy was upset. He was old enough to understand and was beside himself with worry. After the safe delivery of the little sister, he became ill with the flu and stayed home. The teacher recommended that the mother spend extra time nurturing and loving him, reassuring him that all was well. He came back to school much more quiet, calm and ready to study. His healing was amazingly quick.

You cannot hide a family problem from your children, no matter what age they are. They sense it. Even though they are not able to verbalize it, they are aware on some level and react in some way to it.

During the time of the trauma the child can be called upon to help heal the problem through family prayer. Prayer works not only to heal the problem but it heals the one praying as well as bringing calmness, trust and soul growth to everyone concerned. We miss a great opportunity when we do not use the child's powerful healing abilities.

On the higher level, the parents' and child's use of the Spiritual Mind Treatment is a very powerful aid to rise above the appearance to the level where the healing is already a reality. A general treatment for any situation is:

I realize that God, Infinite Power, Perfect Right Action, Universal Intelligence and Supreme Loving Kindness is the total expression of my life and _____ (child's name) _____ life. We unify our thoughts, body and actions with God Consciousness. I recognize that (child's name)_____ is God's perfect expression and that his (body, life experience, mental attitude, etc.) reflect his true nature and he is instantly healed of all appearances and is about his Father's business. With great joy and thanksgiving, I release him to God's Healing and Loving Power. And so it is.

The use of the Spiritual Mind Treatment has been known to bring temperatures down, enable youngsters to breathe, bring the right doctor who knows exactly what to do in this situation. <u>Practice using it before there is a crisis.</u>

The powerful use of the White Light to surround that child, repelling all danger or injury, is available for the parents' protective use. Many accounts have been given of its use by parents of teenagers who have taken the family car for the evening those teens have avoided dangerous situations. It certainly beats sitting home and chewing your nails and worrying every minute that they might have an accident. This is something you can do while you wait that is beneficial to both of you.

Remember that you are never alone. If you are unable to see over the situation or clear your mind of the problem, call your local Religious

Science Church. If there is none nearby call:

The Ministry of Prayer
United Church of Religious Science
P.O. Box 75127
Los Angeles, CA. 90075
(213)385-0209

All the help you need is activated as you turn to God expecting a healing.

YOU ARE GOOD

A lady in her eighties said to me, " I long to hear, YOU ARE GOOD! You are a good girl."
If that is true of people in that time of life, so must it be true of a child just starting out. Let him hear what his soul yearns to hear. "YOU ARE GOOD! You are kind! You are so good to your little brother. Thank you for helping your sister so nicely. You helped me a lot by helping her, etc."

Our soul needs--hunger and thirst for-- this affirmation. Be the one who says it to your child at the time and later at bedtime during your Soul-to-Soul talk. You are not just touching the mental level. You are opening the inner being and awakening the Divinity within. To develop the action pattern and thought pattern from the Divine Center is an important activity of this life. To be confident that his reflex actions will always come from his highest and best is an important purpose of his life.

Just as thumping the thymus returns you to your Center, acknowledging the child's appropriate act at the time does the same. "Look for the good and praise it" and more good will be the result.

Say " YOU ARE GOOD" often so your child will remember it and not yearn to hear it in later life.

CREED OF THE AWAKENED SOUL

Teach your child to say this, know this and prove this truth to himself. Teach him to understand and use it to its greatest degree

CREED OF THE AWAKENED SOUL

I am a powerful Spiritual Being.

My Power is a part of God Power.

I use my Power with wisdom and compassion.

I merely center myself in the stream of God and let go.

I use my Mind with ease to change appearances in my life and the lives of those whom I influence.

I simply know the highest Truth and it becomes a reality.

I have many abilities, such as: precognition, clairvoyance, clairaudience, power over matter, time and space so

that I may serve God to a greater degree.

I will never abuse my Powers or use them for a lesser purpose than they were designed.

Knowing all this, I still have the freedom to choose to be a great Light Bearer of God, or not.

Always, I remain a highly evolved Divine Spiritual Being of God.
Alyce Soden

DOOMSDAY ATTITUDE

What if the end of the world is tomorrow? What if earthquake, fire or flood, tornado, typhoon or volcano erupts and the earth explodes? Of course, science has no predictions that this is going to happen, but some youngsters may be using the idea of a cataclysm that will end it all to avoid facing life or to live recklessly and carelessly.

In any case it is a "cop out" and don't buy into it, parents. There is no excuse for not living life to the greatest degree and being the best you can be. Stand firm with your child. He has the responsibility to choose and if he doesn't choose, he will reap the effect of race consciousness choosing for him. The Law works that way.

Race consciousness is the collection of all the beliefs of the people of the world. Each country, state, city and neighborhood have a consciousness made up of the collective beliefs of their people. The Law brings to actuality what the sum total of these beliefs are into the lives of individuals. No one is exempt. However, when a person chooses his own beliefs, he overrides race consciousness and brings about what he chooses. So if a person chooses to believe that the world is coming to an end and there is nothing he can do about it, this will be the effect, his reality. He may base his actions upon this faulty premise.

On the other hand, if he decides to change that belief to "I have something important, exciting and beneficial to do", and begins to move in that direction, his reality will change.

Drugs, alcohol, or avoidance of the world are some of the effects of this attitude. And it may take some shock treatment to get that child back on the track. (not electric shock) but it must be done. Spiritual Mind Treatment is a powerful tool to shake this loose. Heal this sense of separation by knowing that God's Love includes everyone, particularly your child and that no inaccurate belief has any power over him. Circle him in God's Love, bless him and know that he is healed, now!

"It is not everyone who merely says to me, My Lord, my Lord, who will enter into the kingdom of heaven, but he who does the will of my Father in heaven." Matt. 7:21

Chapter 12

MASTERING LIFE

TEACH YOUR CHILD TO UNDERSTAND AND USE THE UNIVERSAL LAW.

What is Universal Law? Universal Law is God in action. One Law, the Law of Cause and Effect (Karma) is available for our use every moment of every day. As we use this Law it appears to have many applications. I call these Spiritual Laws Over the millenniam man has uncovered a number of applications of the Law which apply to all people in overcoming appearances and taking charge of their lives. The use of the Universal Law is the most important lesson mankind must learn.

The Law applies on all levels. The level of the physical: body, health, feelings, emotions, self-esteem and ego. The level of the world of effects: food, clothing, shelter, work, prosperity, success, relationships and mental activity. And the Spiritual Level: love, living in God, seeking the highest and best for all, unity and mastering life which is inevitable as the individual evolves.

As humankind evolve, the application of the Law of Cause and Effect becomes a plan, a pathway of the highest form of Spiritual Life. Use the Universal Law and its application consciously and teach your child to do likewise. Learn how to harness God Power (Universal Law) and you will be well on your way to mastering life.

#1 THE LAW OF CAUSE AND EFFECT--KARMA

The Universal Law of Cause and Effect. Karma is really the only Law. All others come from it. What you give out, you get back. If you are filled with fear and suspicion, you will receive back reason to be fearful and suspicious. If you give love and trust, you will receive back loving and trusting actions from others. When our children learn this individually and practice it throughout life as a lesson learned, the world will reflect it collectively. It takes just a few to change the world. A loving and spiritually aware child can go through the hustle and bustle of a day at school and receive the good that is there, hardly affected by any other happening.

When the lesson for your children is: if your child cheats on a test he will get caught, is graphically learned, the embarrassment is far worse than the failure would have been. If he steals another's gym clothes, his will no doubt be stolen. His attitude about life is the cause, not his parents' attitude, or his friends' acts. He will experience the effect in some way. So don't try to blame anyone else. He must take the responsibility for his acts, think before he speaks, and consciously place good ideas into his mental pattern. Then the effects will be good. You can depend on it. It is a Law. This may seem simplistic, but it all depends on your child, himself, the individual.

II THE GOLDEN RULE

DO UNTO OTHERS AS YOU WOULD HAVE THEM DO UNTO YOU. And do it first and all the time.

Matthew 7:21 (R.S.V.) "Whatever you wish that men would do to you, do so to them."

Udana-Varga: "Hurt not others with that which pains yourself."

Mahabharata: "This is the sum of duty, do naught to others which if done to thee, would cause thee pain."

This ancient rule is found in some form in all the world Bibles. It has been taught by the enlightened souls of the ages and is a mutual heritage of all peoples. It remains one of the first and most important Laws that children must learn. If you don't like to be hit, don't hit. If you don't like to be kicked, don't kick. The same with biting, pushing, spitting, stealing and all other aggressive behaviors. Children from ages two to five need to understand and master this Law. The parent may have to physically illustrate if the child persists in the habit. Appropriate behavior on how to get along with others must be learned at the sandbox stage of life. (Some world leaders have not learned it as yet.)

This must be obeyed in dealing with others throughout life, as any action given out will always return to the sender.

In teen age, the lesson can be devastating. Don't gossip, or you will be gossiped about. If a person wants to be your friend and you are not interested, be gentle. Let him down as easily as possible. The same could happen to you the next time. Be friendly to all people, and they will be friendly to you. Danny Kay was a prime example of this Law. He went about the world loving and being friendly especially to children and received much love in return. A smile and a friendly word go a long way when a child is feeling strange and alone. Teach your child early that all-----ALL are God's children. All races, creeds, nationalities and colors are the colors of God. Teach your child to recognize God in everyone he meets. Treating others as he wishes to be treated will prepare him well to walk anywhere in the world unafraid and protected.

III THE LAW OF MENTAL EQUIVALENTS

Teach your child to imagine at an early age. Pretending can fill many happy hours. Learning to visualize is the next step. A lady said to me, "I can't visualize." "It's a lot like pretending. Did you learn to pretend when you were a child?" I offered. "No, my parents thought it was foolishness so I never learned" was her sad reply.

How true, at one time some people thought pretending was harmful. " Never mind," I told the lady. "You can catch up. Pick a book of beautiful pictures and look at one. Think what it would be like to be there. Don't just see it, feel it. Feel the wind blowing, the sun warming you, and before you know it, you'll be visualizing." A person who has learned to pretend can build castles, overcome any pitfall or problem, and make a happy life out of an austere or barren existence.

Developing a good imagination is an important step in consciousness and vital for the creative professions such as architect, engineer, artist, writer or hairdresser, as well as many others. It is a basic step in using the Law of Mental Equivalents. We use it whether we know it or not. We visualize in our minds how to get where we want to go by reading a map or how to arrange our dresser drawers in an orderly fashion. So don't believe that you can't visualize.

Secondly, the Law of Mental Equivalents works this way. What you see in your mind's eye is what you get. The pictures you hold in your mind are what's outpictured in your world. We are creators, too. We create our lives and the people who come into and go out of them.

You may ask, of the generation who grew up on the television series Life With Father and Father Knows Best "Why didn't that group of youngsters' lives turn out as calm, ordered and caring as those stories were?" Some did turn out similar to the programs, but usually there was some adult standing by saying, "The real world isn't like that," particularly when they had just had a fight with the spouse, or brought home a "new" mother or got drunk for the fun of it. So the child held in his mind that TV stories were a pipe dream and couldn't really happen. Of today's TV offering of partying, soaps, violence and high speed chases, the parents have to say, "The real world is not like that," either. What is a child to believe? He will believe the example set before him in his own home. The Mental Equivalent he holds in his mind will be the truth for him, WILL BE THE TRUTH FOR HIM.

The way it works: The Universe merely says YES and acts upon the picture in his mind. It does not judge nor rearrange anything. It merely acts. Help your child to see that if he holds a picture in his mind of his getting 100% on his math test and does his part of studying his lesson faithfully, it will become a reality. World sports champions in tennis, golf, basketball and others have discovered that a half hour visualizing their action in the game is more beneficial than an hour practicing. Many believe they won and became champions as a result of using visualization.

Pictures held in the parents' mind of desires and expectations for their child contain great power. When the child can likewise adopt those or similar pictures for himself, they will become a reality. When do you stop making the pictures as a parent? When the child takes over. There is a point in time when the parent lets go and releases the child to his greater good, no longer specifying, but blessing. Visualization provides great power and will bring about the fulfillment of the greatest good.

What is contained in a picture or mental equivalent? Make the picture complete.
Include health, relationships, success, happiness, peace of mind, living in a beautiful

and wholesome surroundings and living up to his highest calling. This you can do for your child for his entire life without meddling. Do this kind of blessing daily and you will see the result graphically in his life situation. And do not give up if it is not immediately forthcoming. He may have put some pictures of his own into the Law that have to be lived through first.

Mental pictures of God's purpose for your child are powerful life-shaping molds that will eventually come into fruition. Know it, treasure it and keep it in your heart. IT IS THE TRUTH!

IV THE POWER OF LOVE

Teach only love and life will reflect love back to you. LOVE POWER IS GOD POWER, pure and unadulterated. It is the energy of which all was made, the earth and everything on it. When your motive is love inspired, you can ask the greatest gift; your response is the greatest you, you can be. No greater gift can be given than love. True love given freely cannot be taken back and goes unerringly to its intended. When parents are separated or divorced, one parent may feel that he does not or cannot love his child and may use his influence to get back at his former mate. This is not true love given freely. True love has no strings attached and is given regardless of the circumstance. It seeks nothing in return but love.

Love is the natural givingness of babies to all and they will continue to love as long as the world around them expresses love to them. A sheltering home, which every child deserves to have, will sustain that natural expression for a lifetime.

It was through love energy that your child was brought into this world. It is love that sustains him throughout all lifetimes and brings him home to unity again with God. It is up to the <u>important persons</u>; the parents, family members, teachers, and friends who influence the childs' life to add their love to that being. This is not to say one has to be a push-over and accept any kind of behavior from your child. Not at all. Allowing this is a disservice to the child and others. Expecting the highest and letting the child know when he is performing inappropriately is always your responsibility as parents and family members.

When did you say " I love you," to your child last? Do you make it a regular practice? No matter how old he is 2,10 or 60, start saying "I love you" to him and you will begin to hear it coming back to you for the rest of your life. Love begets love.

Some people rarely say "I love you." It's as if they have an obstruction in their throat when they might want to say it. Consequently, they don't hear it very often either. Don't let your child grow up not knowing that he's loved. His guessing that you love him or having to search for evidence in your actions is not the same.
Tell him often and show him, too. Knowing that he's loved makes a much more secure child, and a stronger base of security means he'll not go about the world seeking love desperately so desperately that he makes poor choices as a

God's Limitless Love showers us endlessly.

Illustration # 2

The power of Love overcomes all negative emotions such as: anger, fear, hate, and worry. There can never be a limit to God's love, only our willingness to accept.

result. A young woman said,"I was so starved for love, I gave my body to anyone who wanted it. Consequently, I became a mother at age 14".

Teach your child about the Circle of Love Law. Starting with the child giving love first to himself, then to his parents, brothers and sisters, his grandparents, his pets and his friends. Then let him extend his Love Circle to his classmates and neighborhood as he grows older.

Point out how his love goes out and comes back to him multiplied. The more he gives out, the more he receives. Love actually revolves in circles. Begin a Love Circle with him so he feels what it's like to give love and receive love. This will alleviate that common adult problem of not knowing how to give or receive love or how to act when it's given.

Study chart No.II God's Love Circle, and you will see that the more love you give, the more your receive.

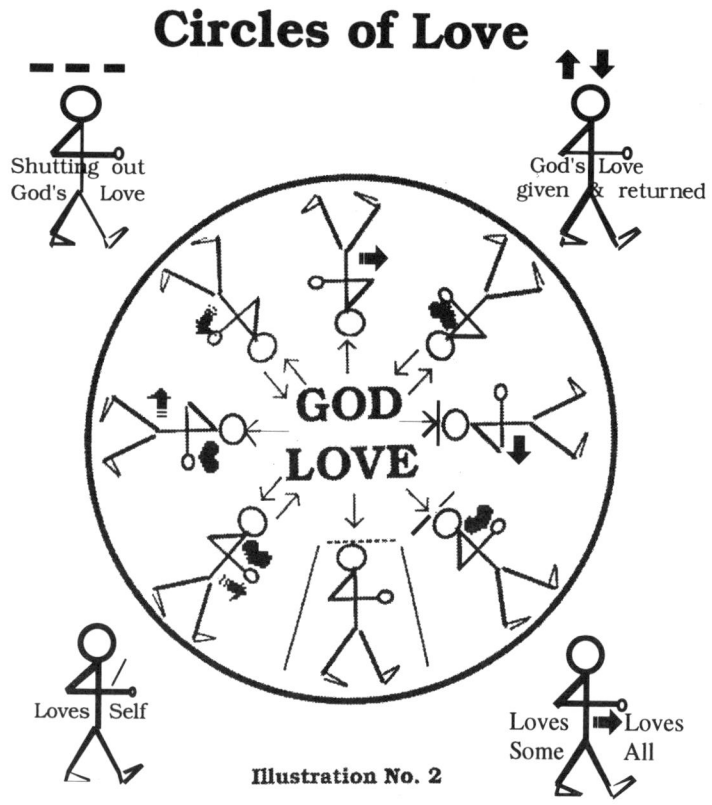

Illustration No. 2

Lessons to be noticed in God's Love Circle Chart

1. You can't out give God. God will give to you whether you accept it or not.
2. You can choose not to give or receive love from anybody, including God, for any reason: not worthy, afraid there are strings attached. That is your choice. But God will always give to you.
3. Perhaps you are selective, and give love to some but not to others. This is possible.

4. You can be a part of the Love Circle by accepting the love, God gives you and pass it on, in which case the love to you increases both ways.
5. The choice is always yours consciously or subconsciously.
6. LEARN TO BE A PART OF GOD'S LOVE CIRCLE AND TEACH YOUR CHILD TO DO LIKEWISE.

So Jesus said to the centurion, Go, let it be done to you according to your belief. And his boy was healed in that very hour. Matt. 8:13

Chapter 13

THE LAW OF BELIEF
#V IT IS DONE UNTO YOU AS YOU BELIEVE

This Law, an adaptation of the Law of Cause and Effect, was given by the Master Jesus to define the power of the mind. The mind of each individual has ability to make and shape one's world. Your child, starting early in life, knowing this Law and being experienced in using it, will be able to program his life and accomplish much in his lifetime.

Start as simply as you can. The child's favorite toy is broken. The child is unhappy about it. Together, declare that somehow it will be fixed or replaced. (Resist the temptation to rush out and buy a new one or repair the old one.) When the question of that toy comes up, declare its wholeness. Believe it, know it. Watch for the way it will come about. When it is accomplished, remind the child that the Law "It is done unto you as you believe" has acted. It was done as your child believed.

Some lessons such as this have to be repeated over and over again throughout the lifetime to make them a learned, dependable method of operation.

An older child wants to visit his grandmother, but there is no money available. Use the Law of

Belief involving a simple Treasure Map. Put a picture that represents what he wants in a place where he will see it and affirm that he wants it, he deserves it and he will have it. Remind him that the Law has acted on his belief when it comes about.

There is nothing more effective to remind you of the actions of your belief than by keeping a record. Keeping a diary of the specific demands that you make on the Law is a powerful faith builder. When you have named your desire and dated its fulfillment, you have evidence that the Law works and it will work on any need or desire that you may have. An easy plan is to make a scrapbook with your child using pictures cut from magazines or newspapers. Sharing with your child when you have a desire fulfilled is excellent and builds a closeness, a trust that is life long.

VI THE POWERFUL LAW OF THOUGHT

Ernest Holmes taught that "thoughts are things and you can change your life by changing your thought." Our thoughts have power in every conceivable way. They are creative and they contain energy within them to make what we think come about. By guarding our thoughts and keeping them always on the good and the true, positive and successful, we can confidently know that only good will come to us, as only good is coming from us.

Teach your child to pay attention to his thoughts. If he thinks he's a failure, he will be one. If he thinks he's a success, he will be a success. If he's afraid of that bully child at school, he'll set it into motion and the energy will cause a confrontation.

Life's experiences sometimes bring about an experience that causes one to think they are less than they are. Let's wipe can't from our vocabularies and replace it with can. I can if I think I can. Reading the classic story of The Little Engine That Could at a very young age can form a fine mind set pattern for the child. It is not uncommon for a child to meet something that he can't just fly over, that takes work or effort on his part to master such as the multiplication tables. When this challenge comes, both parent and child need the persistence of the little engine to do what is necessary to master the problem. Much is learned in the mastery of any problem, even the most mundane, that is life molding. Resistance, blaming others and avoidance are learned if the problem is not mastered.

The thoughts a child goes to sleep with at night are very important. Choose carefully the stories that you read at bedtime. Make bedtime a peaceful and pleasant time of loving and caring.
Make going to sleep a soul-revealing time. The child is very open at that time to life-shaping thoughts. Return often to the pathway he has chosen in this life. Take that time to reaffirm his purpose here on this earth, to assure him of your love and God's love always supporting him. Look at the happenings of the day and instead of confronting his actions that were not acceptable, explore different, more positive ways of handling them in future. Use the time to

reestablish your bonds and guide him further along his way.

Negative thoughts about one's abilities never make a champion. Sometimes you may feel like a football coach lifting the negative thoughts of a losing team at half-time. But be that, and do what is needed. Take whatever time it takes to bring about a feeling of being loved and blessed for your child. Remember, you will not walk this way again. The opportunity will never be quite the same.

When your youngster has to face a difficult situation like going to the dentist or doctor, play a 'I Am Thinking Game' along the way. I am thinking the doctor will say,"We'll take the cast off today." Or the dentist will say,"No cavities." Setting the mind into pleasant and good thoughts make that action a reality and also takes away the fear that might cause other reactions.

Learning to use positive affirmations will help mold his thought powerfully to the good. Teach him to say:"I am a good boy, I am a healthy boy, I am careful with others and give them love.
I am kind to animals. Let him make up some affirmations that he needs to work on and make a poster or chart for his bedroom. Most parents would like: "I am neat and tidy. I pick up my toys and put them away when I'm through playing with them. I am proud of my neat and clean room."

Remember, you are building thought patterns that will stay with him for a lifetime.

Make them count!

On the higher level, patterns of thought, ideas or plans are already implanted within his innermost being. They will be revealed as he matures. Encourage him to look within himself. Encourage him to seek, listen and watch for the answers to puzzling questions for which you have no answer, he does: such as questions about his future. He can ask daily as he is dozing off to sleep and the answer will come in some wonderful way. Make a note of the answer.

Thoughts are things and have power to shape your child's life. Teach him how to use his mind for his benefit as a means to bring about a fulfilled life.

VII TO THINE OWN SELF BE TRUE

Shakespeare gave this important Law:" To thine own self be true and thou canst not then be false to any man."

Find a reason to teach this Law while the child is still in elementary school as it will lead him gently and surely through the trials of the teen age years.

To discover its truth takes some soul searching and reflecting on the child's part to uncover what would be the highest and best for him in the situations that are presented in his life. In the day-to-day jostle of action and interaction at school, children learn how to act or react to stimuli usually by trial and error. When a youngster sorts out what is the best for him and holds to that, he will discover the power it holds for the good for all concerned. Question: Does telling the teacher that Joe is beating up on him on the way home from school, being true to himself or squealing? Bring this question up for discussion. You will be surprised at his answer. Help him reveal to himself what would be the highest and best for him in the situation and then, holding fast to that, set forth with faith and courage to master it.

Making a simple list of his desires is a good beginning:
1. Be a friend to everyone.
2. Be well thought of and respected.
3. Be able to have the freedom to do his work at school without fear.
4. Enjoy a few friends.
5. Be able to participate freely in school activities.

Help him to understand that these desires will not be possible for him if he is not willing to let others have the same rights. He must be:
1. A friend to everyone.
2. Think well of others and respect others.

Where does he learn respect? At home, of course! He learns respect by being respected. When you borrow from his piggy bank or his new tool, ask his permission and return whatever you borrowed. When he needs to change bedrooms with his sister(for whatever reasons) respect his opinions, and so on. REMEMBER: CHILDREN WHO ARE RESPECTED, RESPECT OTHERS.

Being a "bully" shows that he lacks respect for himself and others. Being a bully or being bullied are two parts of the same thing. Whichever side your child finds himself on can be conquered by further study of this Law. If your child is the bully, you will probably not hear of it from him, or he will claim that someone is bullying him. Watching him play with his friends unobtrusively may reveal the truth. Help him reflect on his feelings of himself. Does he feel good about himself? What can you do together to help him feel happier and more accepted by others? Inner sharing of this nature often heals the matter completely.

If your child is being bullied, question why he is letting someone take away his right of free choice? Decide between you what action should be taken. Make a list of the good qualities you can see in this individual. Anticipate and affirm that the child in question will treat your child expressing those good traits, always. A little love and friendliness will go a long way toward healing this ill will.

In the teen age years, it seems that everything is magnified. The question of following a gang appears. Some youngsters fall into the trap before they know it, just going along being friendly. Sexual promiscuity, breaking the law, drugs and alcohol are often the initiation rights for joining a gang. You may not know when your youth is being faced with this choice. But your best precautionary measure is to examine this question in your quiet times together. Start before your child is in his teens.

Questions to reflect on are, for example: Will I be true to myself if I become a gang member and do what is expected of me? Do I think that the gang will have no influence on me? What is it that my highest self requires of me? How can I live in this world, get the most out of my school time and not be affected by what goes on with my friends?

Pay most attention when he shares with you what some other person is doing. It may be his way of getting the direction from you that he needs. Keep the avenue open for discussion even if you feel that it's already too late. Stay with your teenager and support him in every way. You cannot be with him, guarding, guiding and protecting him all the time, but God can and is. Use your ability to surround him in White Light. Teach him to do likewise.

You may discover that your child is being well protected as one mother did by the White Light when her son injured his foot and was at home soaking it, while his "friends" robbed a sporting goods store. This really happened. The gang was caught and spent some time in jail. The mother was eternally grateful and the youngster learned a great lesson. He never gave away his power of choice again. The Universe protects its own pure seed.

Parents, don't give up. Continue loving and blessing and expecting to see revealed the true highest self your youngster can express.

VIII   THE POWER OF THE WORD

A time will come to teach your child the Power of the Word. When it comes, you can explain that each and every word has power to bless, to heal, to send love and to receive love. On the other hand, it can also curse and bring about unhappiness and non-acceptance of others. Our word has power in every conceivable way. It is the outward indication of what our inner mind-set is focusing upon. When a child says: "I can't, I can't, I can't," that is where his mind-set is at that time. That does not mean it will not change, even though we may believe thoroughly that it won't.

"I can't do this math. I can't learn this poem. I can't draw. I can't make friends. I can't sing." All the <u>can't</u> need to be changed to <u>cans.</u> And you may well be the one who has to do it. Often children don't even know they have a pattern of saying "I can't" until you begin pointing it out to them. Sometimes just a little of your attention or willingness to help will turn the tide to "I might," then to "I think I can",to "I can!" The more he thinks "he can" the easier the task becomes. Encourage him to say it outloud. Use the power of the word.

Learning is a lifelong challenge for all of us and the sooner we learn how to learn for ourselves, the less confusion or trauma there will be in our lives. I shall never forget the little one who had great difficulty in learning, saying to me one day while on yard duty," I'm going to get brains tomorrow. They'll just take my head top off and put some in." (She was to see the psychologist the next day for special testing.) I wish it were that simple.

How often do you hear adults say: "Computers, they scare me. I don't know what I'd use one for in my business." Children have new tasks, procedures and methods presented daily at school that they are expected to master. We demand a great deal of them. Children have to learn constantly to get along in this world. Watch for mind-set blocks that your child sets up to avoid learning . Allow him time to change his mind from "I can't" to "I can!"

A mother came to me very worried. She had overheard her thirteen-year-old daughter swearing like a trooper while playing with her friends in the back yard. "We just don't talk that way in our home. She must be learning that from her friends. I felt like washing her mouth out with soap and making her get some new friends," the mother threatened angrily.

As we talked, she calmed down. I felt she had done well not to do anything at the time, not to even let on she knew. Thirteen-year-old girls are tricky at best to reach and to change them in any way takes careful strategy. " Do you have a quiet time regularly?" I asked. "No," was the reply.

"Start taking time to talk on things of interest to her and begin to listen. Teen age will go much better for you if you start sharing your ideas now." I shared.

"I work. I'm tired when I get home. Then I have

to get dinner, clean the house. Check on the other children's homework. That's too much!" she exclaimed.

"Do you sit down and rest later in the evening?"

"Well, yes I do."

"That's the time to have some good sessions. Do not try to cover too much ground at each one. Remember, that you are molding a life, not pruning a tree."

"How do I handle this swearing business?" she asked.

"Teach her that 'thoughts are things' and the words we use are a law unto our life. If we curse someone, we will be cursed. If we say unkind things about someone or to someone, it will be returned to us"the chickens come home to roost." More important than solving the actual problem is to build confidence between you so when something of greater importance comes up there is a way to handle it."

The mother went away very doubtful, but later reported back that she asked her daughter what she thought of someone who swears.

Wise thirteen-year-old daughter, she knew just what to say. "Jeanne and Jo swear all the time and it's awful."

Mother asked, "Do you really think it's awful?" Awful enough to set a good example for them and the rest of your friends? Should you play with someone that awful?" questioned the mother. "You are the leader of your group. What you do others will follow,"

This was a start in the right direction but more listening and less confronting proves to be a better method.

The true inner self will be revealed when the parent is truly listening and working on the problem. Children often have strong emotions that they do not know how to express. This is where a team approach is very beneficial.

A friend of mine had four daughters. Her husband had died when they were small so it was up to her to raise them. Her second daughter had a terrible temper. Almost anything would set her off. Try as she would, this mother could not get any change in her behavior. They spent much time in-between explosions talking about the cause and sought other means of action and reaction. "We used a secret signal between us to help her use other ways of reacting, When I noticed the signs coming on,
I'd give her the signal. We tried various methods but counting to five then consciously breathing, and counting on to ten, and breathe again until the trauma had passed helped the best." the mother shared."People always said, My what well behaved daughters you have!"

"That is true because we worked on it. I took their words and their outer behavior as indications of how they felt within. I listened until I understood and then we made a plan to change that feeling and that response."

Our words have the power to reveal thought patterns and feelings, and we as parents need to be aware of what our child is thinking, feeling and where his interests lie.

If your child is having behavior problems at school, request that he be put on a daily contract with a simple report from the teacher going home each day. Make him responsible to get the report, bring it home and return your reply the next day. DAILY, talk with him about the happenings of the day and his feelings about them. How did he feel and act? Let him know exactly what you expect of him at school: sit down, be quiet, do his work, be friendly to his teacher and get along with the other students. When he succeeds, lives up to your expectations, celebrate with him. Expect him to behave his best at all times and he will. Likewise, his classroom adjustment will be excellent and he will succeed in school. The main secret, parents, is to start early in his school life. Have high expectations. Don't wait until there is a problem. His teacher wants him to be happy and problem free and will cooperate if you approach in the right way with a plan.

Behavior problems are an outward expression of confusion within. Usually, a confusion of what's expected by the parent and the school. Whatever the problem is, you can solve it together and bring peace to the inner child. When it is so on the inner, the outer world will reflect it also.

Having a behavior problem is not necessarily an indication of the child's soul level. How wisely he deals with his inner confusion indicates his level of enlightenment. Coming into this life from another time period or another culture may be a bit of a shock, bringing about this maladjustment and poor behavior for a time. I'm sure Huckleberry Finn might have some adjustments to make were he to reincarnate in this time! When the problems are "outgrown," so to speak, and his behavior under control, his true higher self will shine through

Remember: There is one Universal Law, the Law of Karma, Cause and Effect and there are Spiritual Laws which correspond with it.

The Spiritual Laws we have discussed are:
1. The Law of Cause and Effect, Karma.
2. The Golden Rule. Do unto other as you would have done unto you.
3. The Law of Mental Equivalents.
4. The Power of Love.
5. The Law of Belief.
6. The Powerful Law of Thought.
7. The Law of Being True To Yourself.
8. The Power of the Word.

This seems quite overwhelming. So many Laws to learn about. Actually there are more than these. Never mind! As your child walks through life you will notice the many and varied experiences that bring about the lessons. Soul growth is inevitable. That's our true purpose in every lifetime.

"If it is the purpose of this childs' life on earth to become more like God, then it is your responsibility as his parent to help him reach this goal." Alyce Soden

Chapter 14

PURPOSE OF LIFE

What moral and ethical values are we here to practice and teach? Moral and ethical values have become "outdated" as the church has become a forgotten entity; although the church, once the bastion of ethics, is no longer a viable force, moral and ethical values must be taught. Youth and their parents desire it greatly. When they see and experience the effects of unethical conduct-- favoritism, abandonment and unfaithfulness they question, "Is this the way it is? Is this what the world is all about?" And they have good reason when the priest takes liberties with the beautiful innocent young girl in his parish, or the Boy Scout Leader tries to sell drugs to his scouts, or his school teacher is an unwed mother.

We will not decry the way it is in the world, but will suggest some of the values we need to perfect in this life and ways of presenting them to your youngster.

Fairy tales have been a traditional means of teaching values. Grimm, Hans Christian Anderson and Aesop have survived because of the values they teach. Regular reading and discussion of the main moral and ethical ideas underlying of each and its application in today's life is of great value.

Reading regularly biographies of people who have shown a particular value in their life and action make such accomplishments more attainable to children. There are plenty of heroes from the past and present to steer this generation onward. Parents must consciously set out to provide guidance or children will believe in the negativity which they observe in the streets, that this is the way it is or has to be.

Life-shaping values are often taught haphazardly. When the family gets together to share the news about family members, how often does it get into the negative about who did what to whom? Usually, the party talked about is not present, but the gossip goes on anyway; and the children are nearby, supposedly playing, but their ears are wide open, and little is missed. Values are taught through idle gossip, sad to say, and children are strongly affected by it. Families who have the unwritten rule of never repeating unkind gossip or talking about those not present are on the way to preventing problems.

We had a rule that when we visited a friend or some family members we focused our attention on them and their world. We did not bring up past problems or differences they may have with other family members. We did not carry tales or take sides. We planned a positive agenda of sharing ideas, common interests, experiences, celebrating together the special abilities of each child and giving an opportunity to brag or show off in a loving, supportive family setting.

This is much better than overhearing your aunt say that you remind her of Uncle So and So who ended up a bum. You never forgot it.

How do you handle it when some caring adult reports to you that they observed your child stealing? I've had many kinds of reactions from parents: "Mind your own business!" "Ho, ho, ho, boys will be boys." "He'll out grow it."Or, the child returning the next day with blisters on her hands; Father decided to teach her a lesson, so he put her hands on a hot griddle and held them there. Ethics through cruelty?

Why not just let the school teach moral and ethical values? Why not? The school tries, but if none are taught at home, and there is no follow-up at home, the lessons are not learned. Usually, values are learned from the peer group. You may be lucky and live in a neighborhood that is untouched by the world, but I wouldn't count on it. Moral and ethical values that are taught at home and enforced at home shapes lives, no matter the kind.

How to go about teaching moral and ethical values? I believe in family discussions on subjects of this importance. During these the parent sets the stage, telling a mythical situation and letting the child discuss what should be done from his way of looking at the situation. Remember, there are many ways to peal an apple. Usually for any situation there are myriad solutions. During these sessions, the parent does well to listen and learn the values the child is discovering in the world.

*Prayer is a powerful life shaping tool.
Teach your child to pray. Alyce Soden*

Chapter 15

PRAYER AND MEDITATION

What is prayer? Why teach children to pray? Prayer works! Prayer for realignment with God, works. Prayer to clear away confusion works. Prayer is talking to the God within. Talking to the God within all day tends to keep our thoughts elevated from the appearance or supposed reality and keeps us in "Heaven." The same is true for our child.

Prayer is not beseeching or begging a fickle God, nor changing God's mind about anything. God is changeless; the same yesterday, today and tomorrow. God has already given all and continues to give all to Its creations. So prayer must be a realignment of man with God. God is never and will never be separated from us, though in our freedom of choice we may feel separated from God at times. So praying to realign one's self with God's love, blessings, creative ideas and protection holds great power. Prayer used as a blessing is a powerful non-interfering prayer to use when your child is grown and you want only the highest and best for him.

YOU ARE NEVER ALONE, EVER! GOD IS ALWAYS AVAILABLE to you in every circumstance or situation. All you have to do is to ask, believing, and the way will open before you and your child. God wants everyone of His blessed children to be happy, healthy, abundant, successful, moral and ethical to the highest degree.

My mother had some knee pads for protecting her knees when she pulled weeds in the garden. I noticed during my teenage years that they were worn through and she spent little time weeding the garden. I attribute the protection and guidance that I received during that very difficult time to the fact that she prayed without ceasing and wore out two sets of knee pads. The blessed seed must be protected.

IT WORKS! IT WORKS when nothing else does! Don't leave it to chance. Spend time in Prayer and Treatment Work. You will see a positive result.

IT IS THE PURPOSE OF THIS CHILD'S LIFE ON EARTH TO BECOME MORE LIKE GOD. IT IS YOUR RESPONSIBILITY AS HIS PARENT TO HELP HIM REACH HIS GOAL !

Prayer is the basis for building a faith that will last a lifetime. The greatest influence you can have on future generations is to teach your child to pray while he is still on your knee. Develop a faith that <u>it works, and it does change things!</u> The simpler prayer the better to begin,

Beginning Prayers

Bedtime: God loves me. God loves my Daddy. God loves my Mother. God loves my brothers and sisters, friends and pets.

Mealtime: Thank you, God, for this good food. It blesses my body and makes me strong and keeps me well.

Keep the ideas simple, but make prayer a habit. Soon the child will add to it in his own words. Give the child an opportunity to say the blessing in family situations often.

Every parent desires that his children be loyal friends with each other for life. This kind of prayer prayed often will release sibling hostility that may be carried into adulthood to the detriment of loving relationships.

Can I pray for things? This question is not often asked as children pray about anything and everything in their world without boundaries. Leave it that way. There are none. Sometimes getting the thing he prayed for is more graphic and faith building than all the health and happiness in the world. Children just accept health, wealth, and happiness as the natural course of things (which they are). So getting the bicycle he wanted clearly identifies it as a natural response to his prayer. How it came is irrelevant.

Learning that prayer is a two way street. Listening for direction from the God within must be introduced and practiced. Many children who have learned this well have avoided the pitfalls of peer pressure in the teenage years. Children can be taught as early as five years of age to listen to that Inner Guide for instruction.

The child needs to listen to the Inner Guide when his friend invites him over after school so that he will remember to call home first for permission. The Inner Guide, or God, is always available to the one who learns to listen and follow its direction. Children who practice this method are always protected and can go through life unscathed. <u>Parents must do the same to set the example.</u>

What about praying for the BIG things, like the return to perfect health of a loved one? Children's unlimited powerful prayer and faith have healed many life threatening diseases. Dr. William Hornaday (Minister of Founders Church of Religious Science) related that when he was threatened with cancer, he went to the nursery class of his church and said to the children, "Heal me!" The children's clear-eyed, powerful affirmations worked. He lived and served God in this dimension for many years after that. When given instruction, children's firm belief causes miraculous healings to take place.

Heal the little things: a stubbed toe or an argument with a friend. The size of the problem is not as important as the lesson in faith that is learned.

TEACH YOUR CHILD TO PRAY KNOWING:

1. The love and caring nature of God.
2. The inner joy of praising and blessing.
3. The certainty that all prayer is answered.
4. The release of forgiveness.
5. The ever present guidance on the inner level.

6. The ability to change appearances through prayer.
7. The knowledge that he is never alone and need not fear.
8. The belief that he needs to cling to any person, place or thing for security is not valid
9. God is his eternal security.

Children who have not experienced the comfort and security of knowing that they are never alone, that God is always present where they are, surrounding them with love and protection, go through life in a very limited fashion, searching for love and security from the outside world. Sometimes these children hold on to parents or family too tightly. When, through natural law, that person is taken in death, the child becomes like a ship without a rudder.

Build a strong foundation of faith in God during the formative years (ages 4-11) and give your child a priceless gift for life.

Affirm;
"I know that God's love is blessing, guiding and protecting _____ along his chosen path. I affirm that Divine Wisdom councils his every step. Only good comes to him and only good is the expression from him. His every need is supplied, and perfect health is his birthright. In no way can he ever be separated from God's loving care. Thank you, God."

The prayer of acknowledgement of God's purpose being fulfilled in your child is powerful.

Affirm:
"I know that God always guides _____ on peaceful, joyful, plenteous pathways and separates _____ from all that is not harmonious;"
or *" I know the Infinite Wisdom guides and the Universal Power that protects are always present within, around and through _____ . I celebrate _____ 's return to the Father's house.*
Thank you, God.

Prayers of thanksgiving are powerful. The Hebrews in the Old Testament accounts gave thanks to God frequently to celebrate the gifts God had bestowed upon them. We metaphysicians know that giving thanks believing before and after the fact contains great power to bring that good into reality. It is appropriate to teach your child this form from babyhood.

Affirm:
I give thanks for the blessing of good health _____ expresses and I know that this is the Truth about him always

The child can sing: *I love life. I want to live. God wants me to be healthy and happy right now.* **Make up rhymes to say and songs to sing when he appears to be sick.**

The prayer of the Master Jesus, "Thy will be done," of course is the most powerful of all. When one is in confusion, needs direction, or needs the highest and best demonstrated in his life and does not know what that is, use "Thy will be done. As I relinquish my will (ego), God's will and my will become identical.

According to Rev. John Hall, "God's will for us is unlimited happiness, perfect health, satisfying and blessed relationships, success in one's chosen field and all needs met, always."

"Thy will be done" releases our need to experience the effect of the causes we have set into motion. It opens the way for the highest and best for all concerned. When you don't know what is best, use "Thy will be done." This is total release to God's care and keeping. It works always, often in ways you could never have anticipated.

TEACH YOUR CHILD TO PRAY! You will not always be present to pray for him, so make prayer a habit in your life and share its blessings with your child. If you do nothing else for your child, TEACH HIM TO PRAY.

FORGIVENESS

Children need to be instructed in the art and power of forgiveness from an early age so as to release the bumps and bruises that happen in the day-to day-living of a family or at school. The lack of forgiveness is carried into adult life and can bring about mysterious or unexplained accidents that seem to have no cause. Teach your child to forgive and forget daily. This is quite natural to children. Here is a simple prayer that you may find helpful:

God is love and in God's love I can forgive myself and _____ for our argument today. I love myself and I love _____ just as God always loves us. Thank you, God.

Children forgive and forget quite automatically. It is usually the parents who tend to hang on to a slight. Let your child set a good example for you if it is a problem. Be willing to learn new habits.

You may desire to make it a team effort. Do the exercise together. When completed, be certain not to bring the problem up again to your child even if you have not forgotten or forgiven. Repetition of the situation will instill it in your child's mind indelibly. Plant only the good experiences in his memory.

MEDITATION

Meditation is listening with the ears of the God within and seeing with the eyes of the God within. From the simplest form (listening to one's conscience) to communing with God using mantras or names of God, a child can be taught to participate with inner and outer benefit.

When to begin? Meditation can be worthwhile to the mother carrying the child, and she can involve the child by holding her belly and stroking it as she meditates. By using her intuitive communication of ideas, she can communicate with the developing child, resulting in a very secure, calm and welcomed baby at birth. Meditating with baby at the breast or sleeping continues that feeling. Using meditation as a part of the family evening "Lessons in Truth" time (suggested in prior chapters) adds further meaning and depth to the lessons.

If you are starting later in his life, tell him that meditation is listening to God within himself. Your child can do it easily when you teach him how. Start by inviting him to join you for a few minutes. Show him how to sit comfortably and close his eyes. (This may be difficult for some children at first.) Use a flower from your garden. Both of you look at it. Talk about its color, shape, perfume, or just generally define it. Suggest that he take a picture of it with his mind. Then ask your child to close his eyes and visualize that flower. Move it away and ask him to smell its perfume still with his eyes closed. When he has mastered that, try sitting by a pond of moving water. Have him take a picture of it with his mind so that he can describe it to you. Then listen to the sounds. Later have him recall the picture and hear the water sounds. Meditation is essentially listening, so do exercises that involve listening to sounds present or recalled. Meditation exercises are excellent calming down activities after active play. It can be very helpful (if the child has practiced meditation) to meditate after some stressful experience. If you use music when you meditate, it will increase the energy level of the meditation and add to your child's enjoyment as he develops his abilities.

Scientists are now saying that meditation provides lasting benefits to your body. You can begin your child's meditation time teaching him a simple body-relaxing exercise.

EXERCISE: Starting from the bottom of his feet, teach him to tighten his muscles, then relax them. Repeat systematically through out the body. Great benefits are accomplished when he can control the systems of the body. Simple yoga positions will be helpful. See <u>Meditating with Children,</u> by Deborah Rozman.

Meditating can become a life-long joy and is easily learned. Great ideas, life plan and purpose, how to live in this world happily, staying in touch with the God within on all three levels of body, mind and spirit are just some of the benefits.

ON HEALING YOUR CHILD'S WOUNDS

If often appears that our children are wounded by the effects of coming into the world. Remember, the world reflects back exactly the pattern given it. The child and the parent hold the pattern until the child is seven years of age. What are you as a parent fearful about? What pattern have you set into motion for your child to experience? Attitudes held and experienced by parents of their early life can be repeated again in their child's life. If you haven't resolved some negative pattern yet, set about changing that now. Attitudes about beginning school or finishing school can become magnified if the parent did not overcome it themselves. Prayerfully examine your feelings about relationships, estrangements with parents, or dealing with neighbors. Releasing condemnation of yourself will overcome any effect your child might have suffered. The child will be freed and make the fine adjustment that is expected.

We (all humankind) came here expecting to be successful, happy, prosperous, healthy, and confident. That is what is meant in Genesis where it says, "And God blessed them. And God said to them, Be fruitful, and multiply, and fill the earth, and subdue it." Gen. 1:28.

When it appears that there is something amiss in the child's life, the parent needs to examine his life experience.

Do not be surprised if some of the world responses that you experienced as a child and did not resolve come again to your child. You get a second chance. This time use your Inner Wisdom, the God within, and overcome any negative effect permanently for both of you.

What is the purpose of our experience in this classroom called earth? The setting out of the question, the answer to it and the overcoming of it. By using the Principles given in this book. YOU CAN DO IT!

but I do know one thing, that I was blind and now behold, I see. John 9:25

Chapter 16

USING THE LAW OF VISUALIZATION

Treasure Mapping With Children

Treasure Mapping is a form of visual prayer to God, not petitioning , but affirming that God is always giving good things and blessing every person. So every Map should contain words of praise and thanksgiving. Regularly affirming God's presence, power, love and support is the secret.

Treasure Mapping can be used for getting things, seeing oneself as he truly is, improving health, changing attitudes and behavior, or any other good use. Your needs and imagination are the limits. All are equally valid as long as one's highest good is the quest. Because adults have used Treasure Mapping for getting things or changing their life situation, they may expect it to be of interest to their child. When it is not, they lose interest and, in confusion, drop it.

Most children do not know lack of any kind or have any consciousness of a need or desire until after the age of seven years when they visit in their friend's homes. Unless there is an adult opinion voiced, most children believe they are having the best childhood ever. Since they do not know what to expect, they accept their life as perfect. I've often heard people say,We were poor, but we didn't know it. Mother seemed to manage with what we had. When we look back later we know, but at the time we didn't.

Treasure Mapping for things works best for an older child who dreams of something that parents can't or won't give. The teenage girl who lives in the city and dreams of having her own horse, is a fine example. This was the Treasure Map theme of a teenager I once knew. The parents thought it was impossible, but the result, the demonstration, suited both her parents and herself. She got a job cleaning out the stable at the local riding academy near her home after school in exchange for riding lessons. This satisfied her desire.

The greatest use of Treasure Mapping with children is when it is used for personality development and behavior modification. Discovering the self is what life is really about. From day one, along with discovering his world, a baby is discovering himself. This method works well to encourage the child to look at himself and see who he truly is, A DIVINE CHILD OF GOD learning to live in his new body and his new world. Self image, learning how to get along with others, and making friends are purposes to which Treasure Mapping is well suited.

It is said that Benjamin Franklin suffered from personality problems as a young man. He had a poor self-image, did not get along well with others, and making friends seemed to evade him. After a day's work in his brother's print shop, he would retire to the local meeting place (tavern) of the young men of that time. There he sat evening after evening wanting to make friends, but no one seemed to notice him. Or if they did, they passed on to sit at a more popular fellow's table. No matter what he did, nothing worked.

After this happened for quite a time, his active inquiring mind began to wonder why. He began to pay attention to the fellow by whom they always chose to sit. What did he have that Benjamin did not have? What did he do that Benjamin did not do? First, he wasn't buying drinks for everybody all the time. In fact, he rarely did. He seemed to have no more money than Benjamin did and he dressed plainly as did the others. What was it then?

Instead of sitting there and feeling sorry for himself, he began to watch, listen, and made a list of the good qualities that this fellow had:
1. Friendly, really liked people.
2. Gave others attention, really listened.
3. Always seemed kind and tactful in what he said and did.
4. Didn't try to show off or hog attention. Let others share the limelight.
5. Had interesting and creative ideas to share. And so on went his list until he had nearly twenty good qualities.

When he looked over the list, he realized that he had several of these traits, but many he did not have. He resolved to consciously develop those traits one by one until he had mastered all of them. And he did.

History reveals that he was one of the most loved personalities of his time and that he was responsible, because of his positive persuasion, for negotiating arms and troops from the French Court for our fledgling nation during the Revolutionary War.

A youngster having trouble with relationships would be helped by making a Treasure Map with love as the theme, loving himself first and finding reasons to love others as well. A poster with his picture in a heart at the center with words of love and peace is a good beginning. Add later pictures of other children to whom he's being kind, friendly and caring. Great strides in personality development can be made through using Benjamin Franklin's technique with a Treasure Map.

Use a Treasure Map to improve a child's health or overcome a physical anomaly. In the center of the poster, start with a picture of the child when he was healthy and happy. Write words of health, strength, energy and joy around it. Put words of thanksgiving to God for his perfect body, and place it the poster in a prominent place so the child can see it often.

A child with a physical handicap can be helped to overcome the situation or the negative effects to the self-image by using a visual Treasure Map. Use a picture of a person with a perfect body; a sports hero or Olympic champion is great. Encourage him to visualize himself looking like that person and doing what that person does. As the body grows and changes and the understanding of the self becomes greater, he will become more centered and may overcome the physical problem completely.

By studying it daily, focusing the conscious mind and visualizing the desire as a reality will bring about the result you sought.

Treasure Maps can be made in a variety of forms. See more examples in my book. Prosperity Is More Than An Attitude, by Alyce Soden.

For young children, make a book that can be read at bedtime to reinforce at that powerful time the positive ideas for a change in attitude and behavior, or a physical transformation. Use photographs and drawings that the child has made to illustrate his idea, his true self. Call it his Life Time Book. Use his own positive sayings and written affirmations. Use a notebook so that more can be added as time goes by and his understanding grows.

GOAL SETTING

A "Life Time Road Map" (See illustration No. 3) is a fine tool for goal setting. It works well for a little older child when the "What to I want to be when I grow up?" question comes up. "What kind of person do I want to be" and"What kind of life do I want to live?" Be sure to add all dimensions of life to this road map: occupation and the kind of training required for that occupation, benefits, family life-style and living situation, level of consciousness and pathway to God's service, and oneness with God. A Life Time Road Map works well when it is made during those waiting, learning and preparing years in elementary school.

By it's nature it can be added to in adulthood.

A stepladder (See Illustration 4) is a good method to symbolize steps in consciousness or steps along the avenue to success in a chosen field. If numerous degrees are needed to accomplish a certain goal, they should be listed on the steps of the ladder.

For one who is willing to get their Treasure Map off the shelf regularly as a means of building faith in the power of prayer, using a notebook has worked well. If you leave all the various items that you have worked for and received in the book, the history of your successes will be obvious.

Is making a Treasure Map for your family, your child's life, a good idea? or will you be stifling him, usurping his right to free choice? A parent, like God, is always desiring the highest good for his child. In that vein, a Treasure Map is a fine tool. Who else would you trust to visualize a wonderful life for your child other than yourself? So use this fine tool as a blessing for you both. Speaking as one "unto whom it has been done," I have experienced no problems as a result and have accomplished a great deal more in this lifetime than I would have otherwise. My mother made a Treasure Map for each of her children at an early age and kept them up to date. I am eternally grateful!

A chart to hang on the wall of your child's bedroom is very helpful. Put the word "God" on the center of a large circle. Divide the circle into several sections like a wagon wheel. Place words of inspiration and love of God around the outside edges. Inside each section put pictures of a particular desire or need. At bedtime review this powerful symbolic prayer with your child. Or make a whole chart with one theme. Children enjoy making their own Treasure Map. (See Illustration 5)

Please remember that Treasure Mapping tends to open one's mind to greater possibilities. Somewhere on your Maps it needs to say THIS, OR SOMETHING BETTER. With this attitude a parent is more open and accepting of the child's individuality no matter the result and continues to support the child in his individual pathway.

I would be very remiss if I were not to mention the "Refrigerator Door Technique" which my dear husband Jim has perfected to an art form. When he finds something he really wants, but there seems no possible way for it to come about, he gets a picture of it and puts it on the refrigerator door. Every time he passes it he says," I want it, I need it, I deserve it and I have it. Thank you, God!" Soon a way comes for him to get his desire.

In reviewing this technique at a workshop, a mother was enthusiastic about this idea so she shared the idea with her three children, ten, nine, and five years, when she returned home. Then she went out to work in her garden. Meanwhile, her five-year-old son took it to heart, went through a magazine until he found a picture of a little black puppy he had been wanting. He showed it to his mother, and they cut it out and taped it to the refrigerator door, just at his height. As taught, every time he went to the refrigerator he'd pat the picture of his puppy and affirm," This is the puppy I want. This is the puppy I have. Thank you, God!"

It was almost a week before his parents had time to take him to the Pound. When they arrived, there was only one black puppy. And it was the only black puppy they had had in weeks. There are no accidents.

We have manifested many things with this method. Sometimes it involved us doing some extra work in order to generate the money needed. And sometimes not. But it is a tried and true method if you follow the rules.

Treasure Mapping is an excellent tool to alleviate fears of all kinds, by using a picture of the child surrounded in protective light. I am reminded of the classical picture of two children lost in the dark woods, behind them is the light figure of Jesus. Many have carried that vision for a life-time drawing on it when frightened or fearful.

If you have to move, depict him loving the new place and making many good friends. The fear of change will be alleviated.

1. Caution: It must always be for the highest good of all concerned. It must not be used to limit anyone's right of free choice as a teenager might want to have a certain boy or girl for a special friend.

2. ALWAYS STIPULATE; "This or something better" God works in wondrous ways.

Always be alert and open to God's greater gift.

3. Caution: If you change your mind, take it down immediately.

Treasure Mapping is a powerful visual prayer that works. Use it very successfully with your child to solidify his life expression, give clarity to his vision, change negative experiences and personality traits, develop faith in God, as well as to guide, guard and expand his life.

Illustration III Road Map-Goal Setting
Illustration IV Ladder-Goal Setting
Illustration V Wagon Wheel Design

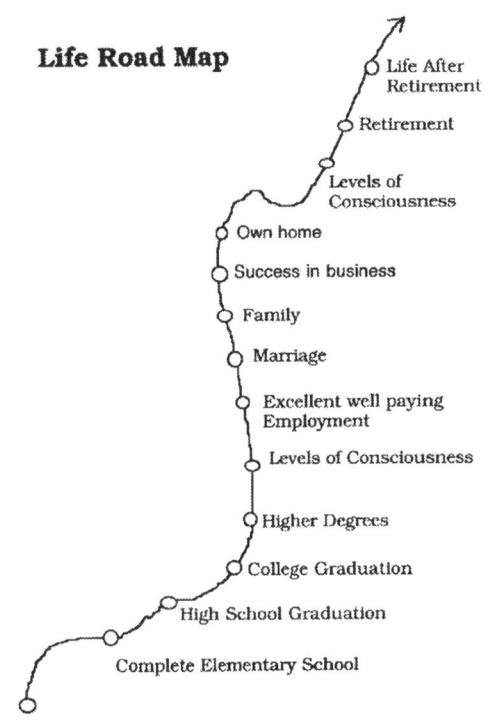

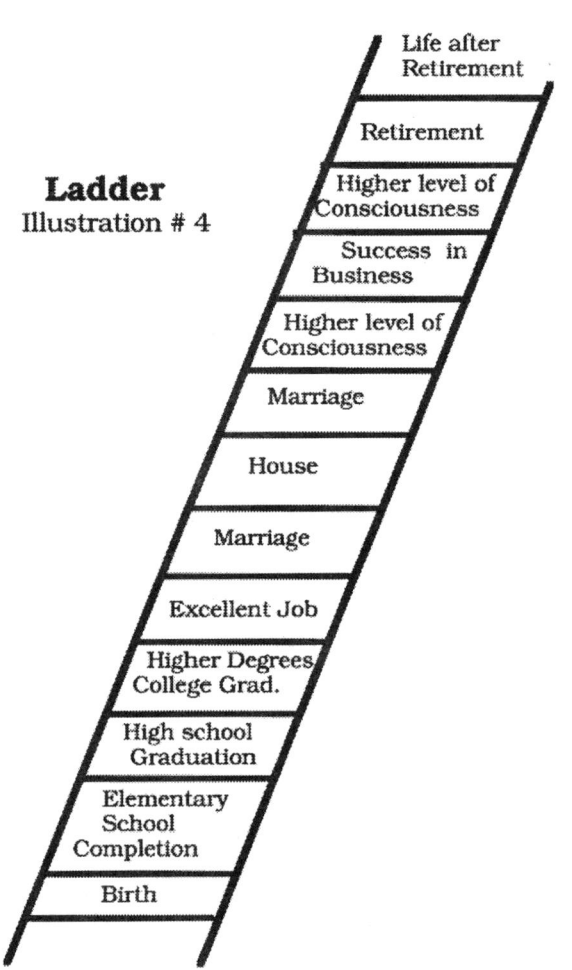

Wagon Wheel Design

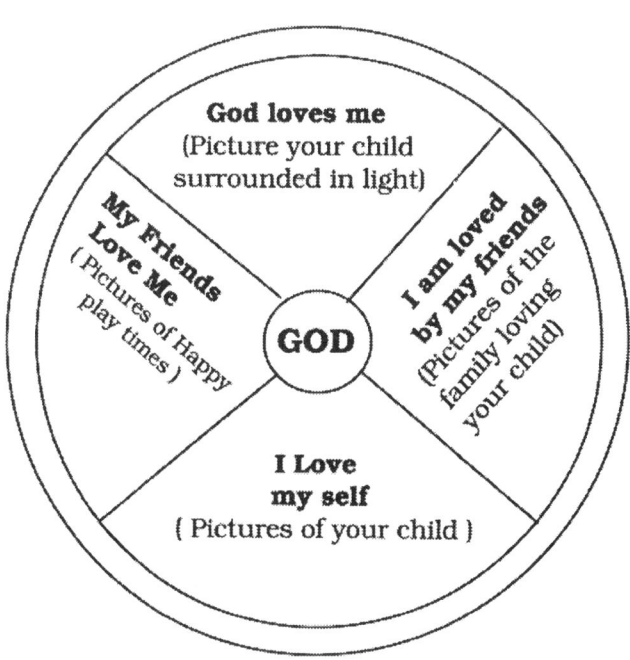

Let your child draw this.

Jesus said to them, Truly, truly, I say to you, Before Abraham was born, I was. John 8:58

CHAPTER 17

FURTHER QUESTIONS

WHAT ABOUT KARMA? Since life is eternal, one physical lifetime is not necessarily independent of another. Souls may incarnate in the same time frame in a family or similar location to bring about a situation that will uplift the consciousness mutually, individually, or of a nation. I do believe that a debt owed in one life time can be repaid in another.

It is my firm belief that all negative Karmic ties are easily severed when one lives in love, peace and harmony. The habit of meeting whatever challenge life presents in a calm, inner, poised manner of confidence always overcomes whatever the appearance. Karmic law must serve the mental level of the individual. The belief in the spiral of all life ever moving upward and onward releases much of the base Karma that we might otherwise carry on from one lifetime to the next. Once overcome, never more experienced.

Mutual ties of love and support may continue over a number of lifetimes as long as it is beneficial to the individuals involved. This is why it is said that the Kennedy brothers are seeking an opportunity to reincarnate together again. Many families remain together for mutual support and individual growth in Spirit, not necessarily in the same order of responsibility-such as mother, daughter, grand daughter, in an order that benefits their mutual need at the time. It appears to generate greater strength of purpose than otherwise when a group reflects the same purpose.

Children who are taught by patient teachers (parents and others) or by example to reflect God qualities in all life dealings will overcome many harmful Karmic debts and will never experience their effect. Race suggestion may not be a negative influence. Often it precedes a dramatic change in mental attitude or life situation. When we can learn from the experiences of others we often do not have to experience it ourselves.

Some children come into the world having difficulty in understanding what is going on and what is expected of them. The child may not have incarnated recently and the impressions received instill an update in behavior, language and social customs needed to function well in this instance. Also, these impressions assist the child when a change in life situation or gender is the case.

We have been taught that the environment a child is born into is the only influence. It is my belief that the soul comes well equipped to live successfully in the life it has chosen with frequent updates of impressions that lend direction, protection and the information needed to reach the goals set for each life experience. These updates may be provided in the form of dreams that direct the child or maybe by helping hands outstretched by living guides.

Race suggestion or world thought just by the strength of its negativity can be alarming to a child coming from the purity of soul. This is the nature of the restlessness of a baby's sleep. Love, comfort and assurance usually overcome his concern.

Premonitions of the things to come are often related by the very young (as are revelations from people of any age). Age may not be the question, but the level of consciousness is more likely the reason. We have heard of a child predicting a plane crash or a house burning. We know that these are always possibilities, but not necessary when appropriate steps are taken.

A premonition can be erased immediately, the script rewritten and the experience thereby altered. Nothing is etched in stone. Children can be taught at an early age to change to the positive any frightening premonitions that come.

When a child relates a frightening premonition, the parent may assist the child to return to the prior events of the dream and change the results mentally. Since all is Mind, the dream change will strongly influence the physical action, possibly alter it completely. Until this is done satisfactorily, the parents should act on the physical level and on the mental level to reduce the possibilities. No premonition, however inconsequential, should by ignored by the parents. Something can be done. As long as the child is troubled by the dream, it hasn't been released and more work must be done.

Remember that this is always in the subconscious state of mind, and the child will often have no recollection of it in the conscious state. Repeated telling of the situation may embarrass the child, and he may be less willing to share the next time. A totally negative response from the parent will seriously undermine the child's confidence in himself and may do irreparable damage to his life purpose. The most helpful attitude is that this is a natural manner of expression. Encourage the childs' freedom to develop his abilities in this area.

REFLECTIONS OF FORMER LIVES

We know that all life is eternal. The memory of former lives is generally veiled from view, thankfully, so as not to influence the present life to any degree. However, from time to time, reflections or memories do reveal themselves in feelings of being familiar with a place or a person. As one advances in conscious awareness, the veil becomes thin and some people are quite knowledgeable of former lives. Children, being closer to the former lives, may be influenced by them by exhibiting great fear when there is no known cause. This may trigger nightmares that relive the reason for the fear, such as when a baby is afraid of water. The sleep directly after bathing may be interrupted by a nightmare of drowning which could have been a reflection of a former experience. Sensitive parents would adjust the amount of water used and not expect the child to sleep immediately after his bath, thus overcoming the fear and laying the reflection of the former life to rest.

ENTITIES REACHING OUT

Entities reach out eternally seeking an avenue of expression or a sympathetic response. These tied to the earth spirits hold onto an idea or object strongly enough to attract a living person's attention. Usually they are of a very low level and not worth even the slightest consideration. However, they may awaken something within a child's memory by an attachment to a former life that needs a response. In this case, an intuitive and knowledgeable parent can reassure the entity and gently release it. In one case a concerned grandfather from the other side sought reassurance that his grandson, Jay, who had just entered this life, was in a loving situation. The present parent gave reassuring messages to the grandfather. He was satisfied and came no more.

We would like to believe that we come into the new life with a clean slate, as one dimensional figures, but such is not the case. We are multifaceted from birth and quite prepared to be successful in the present life experience. Former life experiences and close loving ties do bind us lifetime to lifetime. For generations we have viewed babies as less than human and have set about curbing the animal desire and habits. This limited view has not recognized the hidden agenda, skills, past life experiences, level of consciousness attained and purpose of this present life. Many have been extremely limited by the view that babies are born in sin. World belief has placed great burdens on our young.

Thank goodness it is no longer true in many parts of the world.

PRECOGNITION

A distraught mother came saying,"My four-year-old son is having terrible nightmares and,worse, they are happening in real life. My sister was in an automobile accident just as he described it. She was unhurt but her car was totaled."I explained to the mother, truthfully, that children can get the impression that they caused the accident if the matter is not well handled.

We called Johnnie out from under the serving table, where he was hiding (just finished our potluck lunch after church). " Do you have bad dreams sometimes? " We asked. He looked at us very seriously and said, " Yes, Bad dreams that happen?" we continued He nodded with feeling.
"You have a special gift of God. Try not to be frightened. Just know that you are special. Do you see the white light around your mother?" we asked." Squinch your eyes up and look."we directed. He looked and squinshed up his eyes even more. Then he nodded, "I see it," "Then look and see the white light around me, "I said. He did and then nodded slowly. "Now look at the white light around yourself." He looked as if he didn't believe this, but at last he nodded."That's the white light of protection I put around you. It keeps you from all harm. You can learn to do it, too." "Johnnie, you put a white light around your mother." He looked very serious for a
minute, then nodded. "Now, put the white light around me," I instructed. This took longer. "Now, put it around yourself," which he did. "

Johnnie, when you have bad dreams, put the white light around every person and every thing in that dream. Then it will turn out right. Do you understand what I mean?" He looked searchingly into my face and then nodded and went back to his play.

To the mother I said, "Bedtime is a very important time. Help him practice surrounding those he loves with white light and then going to sleep in a peaceful way. He may still have precognitive dreams but he will be less frightened because he knows how to protect the loved ones involved. He will no longer feel helpless or responsible."

The mother was relieved and very grateful to have her question answered.

PREMONITIONS
What action should be taken as a result of premonitions?

1. An attempt should be made to contact those involved and to warn of the possibility. Warn them to take a different flight, if the premonition is a plane crash or install more smoke detectors if it is a burning house. Whatever comes to the parent as a result of the premonition should be done on the physical level.Remember;this is only a possibility.

2, On the higher level, assist the child who had the premonition to erase the picture by projecting it on a TV screen in the mind and then change channels, or put it on a chalkboard and erase it. Use of visualization is very effective in this instance.

A strong death wish on the part of those involved in the disaster may not be overcome by any act on your part but can be alleviated completely by the persons themselves by decreeing life as their choice.

3. Encourage your child's development of precognitions by giving them credit and acting upon them as if a fact. Precognition awareness is a natural sense that we all have, but few still possess it into adulthood because of our culture's opinion to such things. Parental acknowledgement is all that is necessary. Share any experiences you may have had or relate valid precognitive experiences of others. Make paying attention to premonitions seem normal.

SHINING STRANGER

What should a parent do if a child tells of having conversations with a shining stranger? The biographies of numerous mystics commonly relate early recollections of regular visits and conversations with a shining stranger. Usually the meetings begin in the child's bedroom. Depending upon the parents' reactions, some are moved to a less noticeable place such as a storage room or out in nature, in a tree or by a stream. The purpose of the experience is to further direct the child in the path chosen in the present lifetime. Beautiful poetry or visions of the future are often the result. If the child's early years are sad, lonely or emotionally negative, the shining stranger lends assurance of a future with a purpose, love and blessings. The reassurance may forestall a choice to give up the present life prematurely, as in a crib death or childhood disease or accident.

The purpose for every life is to further the development of the individual soul and increase the level of consciousness of all souls. The individual soul has the right to 'pack it in,' leave this incarnation at any time for whatever reason. And no one has the right to interfere. Crib death or childhood death or any death for that matter is the individual's own choice. When the purpose for this life is satisfied, the choice always remains with the individual soul whether to stay or go on.

If normal precautions were taken, parents need not harbor feelings of guilt or responsibility if the result is a death appearing to be premature.
We do entertain angels unaware. A soul whose purpose is to bring opposing members of a family into a peaceful and harmonious relationship as a result of its birth may not remain long in that incarnation.

This does not mean that we do not do everything we know how to do, or medical science knows how to do, to save that life. That is our responsibility.

WHAT ABOUT THE HANDICAPPED CHILDREN?

Life is eternal. And every life is important in every way. Each experience, limitation or happening in a life is pre-chosen to further the incoming soul's purpose. The soul's development is the main purpose. What about a child born with AIDS? It was that soul's choice, and some will be healed and live normal lives. Those who are parenting such children will grow immeasurably in the love and giving attribute of the soul. It is my belief that each of us has walked the path of physical limitation for a lifetime or more for the purpose of developing some area of soul. And we are never alone. Each is guided and protected by those responsible, such as parents here in life and others responsible for our inner growth on the other side.

ABORTION

The question of aborting a not perfect child is always the mother's unquestioned choice, as is abortion for any other reason. No guilt should be harbored on any person's part. It merely closes a life possibility for that individual soul at that time. Another will be sought and/or the soul may abort itself as a result of another more suitable opportunity. The intended mother may feel strong ties to her aborted child and need much loving counseling to release it to God's keeping, knowing its purpose will be served elsewhere. The soul enters the body at the union of the egg and sperm or anytime there after. There is no sin involved in abortion. There is only choice on either the mother's part or the incoming soul's part.

DREAMS

Dreams for all humankind are a preview and/or review of the life plan agreed to in the present parenthesis. Some precognition and problem solving are incorporated also.

Dreams are vastly underrated in the Western culture. In the Eastern culture, attention is paid to all dreams, and action as a result of a dream is accepted as commonplace. For example, Tevye's excuse for sanctioning his daughter's marriage was accepted by his wife and the community as a result of his dream in the musical Fiddler On The Roof.

Dreams played important parts in the lives of people in the Bible. Two different Josephs at different times were benefited by dreams. Joseph, the father of Jesus, was directed to take his family to Egypt to escape the retribution of Herod. And Joseph, who was sold into slavery by his brothers, interpreted dreams that released him from prison and saved his own people as well as the Egyptian people.

I believe that dreams prepare children for the contributions they are to make in their present life by showing certain actions they must make and preparations they must undertake.

Dreams may reveal the inner pattern forever encased in the soul of their divine nature, always expanding until it reaches its fruition, union with God. A dear friend revealed her recurring dream of a seemingly endless staircase where she is standing on the top step. Would this not reveal a very elevated soul about to ascend?

Dreams can be practical, pertaining to everyday life, as the lady who was having her house built by a contractor. Knowing very little about it, she dreamed of the correct way to set the ridge pole. The contractor was not planning to do it that way. Fur flew!

Recurring dreams should not be ignored, and sometimes the child himself can interpret them if asked. We know that the inner pattern or design for this life is always carried in the soul, so dreams may well be a means to recall it to conscious memory. Parents can use this evidence of preknowledge in guiding the child away from certain life hazards and/or providing the physical instruction to prepare him with the skills needed to fulfill his dream.

Ancient dreamers believed and followed through on their dreams without question and as a result of that trust were able to protect their families. The valuable seed that was put into their care was protected. We need to do likewise. Obey your dreams with regard to your child. They are important.

NIGHTMARES

A parent came asking for help. His daughter regularly seemed troubled during sleep. At four, a child is often incapable of verbalizing what is troubling her. Nightly, or every other, his daughter would awaken crying, unable to explain why. He would hold her, assure her that there was nothing to be afraid of, and she would soon return to sleep.

First, we explored the possibilities. Was it the influence of the world? The father monitored what she saw on TV, the kind of play she participated in and the emotional climate of their home. There was stress and uncertainty. They had just sold their home and moved to a temporary place until their new home cleared escrow. But this did not seem to be the cause. Was she having premonitions of things to come? From what little she said, nothing made sense. The name Ellie that came was unfamiliar to the parent. Still the dreams persisted. Ellie came frequently. So it became clear that the activity going on was not of the child's instigation. So the father attempted to reach through mental impression into his child's dream. By holding her at approximately the same time that the nightmares had occurred, he eventually received a mind impression of what was troubling her. A friend from another life was worried about her as she had been killed in an accident and the friend was searching for her. The father was able to assure Ellie that his daughter was well and happy. There was no need for her concern. He lovingly bid her adieu. She never came again.

Nightmares are a common occurrence in people of all ages. Babies awaken or are restless during sleep. Generally parents need not be concerned, but sleep interruptions that are frequent may need some attention. Some of the possible causes as mentioned before are the influence of race suggestion (world thought), premonition of things to come, reflections of former lives and/or entities reaching out.

Race suggestion has nothing to do with race, station in life, color or creed, but is the strong influence of world thought which permeates a child from birth. Whether learned from the environment or through thought impressions, the opinions of the culture have a strong influence on a child from early on. And this influence does speed up adjustment to the world that the baby is born into, to a great degree. In this view, race suggestion is very positive and helpful in the adjustment of the incoming soul to his new life.

BAD DREAMS

A young mother, on putting her child to bed one night, found her daughter reluctant and uncooperative. This was unusual for a six-year-old, as she was usually cooperative. She seemed quite disturbed. She said." Mommie, I'm afraid to go to sleep. Sally told me all about the devil and witches and that they will come and hurt me in the night. I dreamed about them again last night and I'm afraid to go to sleep."

The mother sat down on the bed and said, "You know that we do not believe in witches and the devil. What do you think would help in this situation?"

"I tried to think good things but I was still

scared." she replied.

"Do you remember how to center yourself in the Light that is within you?" her mother asked.

"Yes." was her answer.

"Let's do it together." the mother offered."Come to that center within you." She touched her lightly on the sternum (center of her chest).

The child closed her eyes and a slight smile came across her face.

"Breathe into that place of peace and let your light shine. Imagine the Light is like a light bulb, shining bright and warm. Let it flow throughout your whole body, starting at your chest and extending all the way to your toes. Let your whole body shine with Light, warm and beautiful. See the Light shining brightly at the top of your head?"

The child nodded. Her smile was even brighter,

"Now, let that light shine bigger and brighter until it fills your room. Feel its warmth and blessing to you? Now let it fill our whole house with its Light. Know that the Light is God's love blessing you and our whole family. Let it bless each person, starting with you. Know that your love blessing is protection and guidance for each one of our family and our pets, too."

The child was noticeably quieter and more peaceful. Her smile radiated.

"Now, let your light bulb shine all around the yard and down the street. See each part bright as day, filled with your light. Now take your black marker and draw a line all around our whole property. Know that our place is filled with peace, love and protection of God and that no bad thing or bad dream can enter."

She is radiant now with light and peace. Her hands extend out to motion that she sees their home place and draws a black line around it.

"You can sleep in peace always knowing that God is guiding, guarding and protecting you," the mother affirmed.

After two times through the old song with a new twist, When You Walk Through A Storm Keep Your Light Bulb Lit, she was asleep.

In the morning the sunlight was not as bright as the happy, skipping girl who greeted her mother. She whispered softly,"No bad dream last night."

For several days, they used this method of going to sleep. Many references were made to keep in mind the idea of the"light bulb." A greater faith and trust in God was developed, plus a method to overcome life's appearances.

SUMMARY

We are all Divine Children of a loving Father/Mother God on the pathway from God to God. Each individualization is a Christ in potential. No one is ahead of any other one, as in a twinkling of an eye all can be transformed.

Our world is the result of our belief. Our attitude is the key. All appearances can and will change when we change our view of them.

At an early age teach your child who and what he is and how to use the Power innately within and he will be prepared to carry the Light throughout his life.

Set aside a regular time for his instruction. Plan the lesson from his present life experiences and share your steps of consciousness, and you will grow together. Learning to take control of his life and surroundings is one of the lessons we all have to learn. The two of you are a powerful majority in mastering life and an unbreakable bond between you will also evolve.

There is only one place he will learn right from wrong and that is from you, his parent. He will learn more from what you do than what you say, but do both. Do, say and be the great example for your child. You are given this opportunity in time to make the most of this life experience. Use it well.

Greater Powers than these will be awakened within each of you as you journey on your pathway. Be open. Accept them as a normal turn of events and he will also. No fear or limited view will occur to impede his journey.

Finally, this precious life force is just passing through. In the time you have with him, show him the way.

WALK ALWAYS IN THE LIGHT!

BIBLIOGRAPHY

1. The Science of Mind
   Dr. Ernest Holmes

2. New Age Bible Interpretation
   Corine Heline

3. Udana-Varga

4. Mahabharata

5. As A Man Thinketh

6. Meditating With Little People
   Cricket Langford

7. Prosperity Is More Than An Attitude
   Alyce Bartholomew Soden